Equal Rights
For
Children

Equal Rights For Children

by

HOWARD COHEN

1980

LITTLEFIELD, ADAMS & CO.

Copyright © 1980
by
LITTLEFIELD, ADAMS & CO.
81 Adams Drive, Totowa, N.J. 07512

Library of Congress Cataloging in Publication Data
Main entry under title:

Cohen, Howard, 1944–
    Equal rights for children.

    (Littlefield, Adams quality paperback series; 350)
    Bibliography: p.
    Includes index.
    1. Children's rights—United States.   I.   Title.
HQ789.C63   305.2′3′0973   80–16005
ISBN 0–8226–0350–0

Printed in the United States of America

Contents

Preface

Equal Rights for Children represents, for me, a standard to live up to as much as an expression of my views about children's rights. It is easy enough to have good intentions, but a good deal harder to put them into practice. Life is full of opportunities to evade, to backslide, and to equivocate. "Not now," "be patient," "wait," are familiar refrains, reasonable enough to adult ears and maddening to children. In writing this book, I have made these phrases less reasonable to my own ears, and, I hope, less reasonable to the reader. Still, "less reasonable" is something less than "unreasonable" and a good deal less than "unfair." I find I need reminders to myself in order to live up to my own beliefs.

It is in this spirit that I ask the reader to consider the argument unfolded here. If children's rights were easy to grant, there would be no need for the painstaking, and sometimes painful, detail. But these rights are hard to acknowledge and even harder to incorporate into a life. By setting my standards in public, though, I am inviting personal accountability.

The invitation is extended, in the first instance, to my children. They are the immediate beneficiaries—standing to gain the most from my adherence to my views. Since I do not parent alone, my wife, too, is greatly affected—she must live with the practical consequences of my adherence to these standards (which are not always her own). Inevitably, my commitments become hers in the eyes of our children. It is, perhaps, also

appropriate that I adopt these standards as a kind of acknowl-
edgment to my parents, who knew how to support my attempts
at freedom—sometimes in spite of their better judgment.

My argument is not focused primarily on the family, and
certainly not on my own. The rights I advocate have broader
social impact than that. In some sense children are confined to
the family—and, of course, to schools. They are not especially
welcome in public when they are unsupervised or in moderately
large groups. This segregation is not official and it is not systematic, but it does indicate that we are talking about the ways
adults treat children—and not simply about the ways parents
treat children. These issues are not private; they have less to do
with family styles than with social policy. Still, for my own part,
the mark of satisfaction in thinking about society is the ability
to bring it to bear on one's personal life. This is more a task
than an accomplishment, for the struggle for children's rights
is only beginning.

I would like to thank those who were kind enough to read
and critique an earlier version of this book for me: Michael
Feldberg, Janet Farrell Smith, Mary Vetterling-Braggin, Richard
Freeland, and John Holt. I would also like to thank the University of Massachusetts at Boston for granting the Sabbatical
leave which allowed me the time to write it.

General Introduction

For at least three hundred years children have been the objects of adult protection. That is, our principal way of relating to children has been to take care of them. This has, of course, not always happened in practice. Plenty of children have grown up abused, neglected, ignored, or left to fend for themselves in one way or another. In spite of this every child, in theory at least, is supposed to spend her or his youth under the watchful and caring eye of some adults. Three hundred years ago this protection was mainly academic: more easily found in books than in daily life. Today child-protection is a well entrenched ideal. It sets the standards for family life and for broader social policy concerning children. Flagrant deviations from it arouse our indignation and sometimes our sense of horror. Protection is our society's official position on childhood; it represents our idea of the best way we can relate to our children.

Yet there are rumblings that our best is not good enough. America's treatment of its children has come in for a fair amount of criticism of late, and much of it does not merely make the point that we have not lived up to our ideals. The ideals themselves are being called into question. Some people are saying that it is time we pay less attention to protecting children and more to protecting their rights. Of course, this does not mean a return to the good old days of ignoring, abusing, or otherwise using children. The point is, rather, that protection alone is insufficient—primarily because it slights children's dignity and diminishes their status. The kind of respect for children which we seek will not be freely given. But if it is to be clutched from grudging opposition, it will have to be demanded; and the demands will have to be supported by rights. This is a difficult and even an uncomfortable thing to say because it carries a not-so-hidden suggestion that we adults are regularly violating children's rights. Even as we protect our children. Even with the best of intentions.

My interest here is not in adding to the criticism of how America treats and mistreats its children. Plenty has been said on this topic. The problems with public education, the juvenile courts, training schools and custodial institutions, the family, and governmental policy in relation to them all have been investigated in considerable depth. It is important that these criticisms be publicized and believed, but it is pressing to have some sense of what to make of them. How are we to respond to the inadequacies of child-protection?

The response I want to develop and defend is fairly straightforward: it is time to extend *all* of the rights which adults in our society now enjoy to children as well. We should abolish the double standard of one set of rights for adults and another—more restricted—set for children. I mean this for all children—all who wish to exercise these rights—and not merely for those who are the most capable, the most intelligent, the most compliant, the "safest." I also mean this for all rights; for everything which has the status of a right in our society. This does not mean that children should be treated as adults in every respect, for not all of our relationships with one another involve rights. But where adults have rights with respect to one another, children should as well. I, as an adult, have a right that certain information about myself will remain confidential as long as I so choose. Children should have that right also. I do not have a right to chocolate cake for dessert or to a new film at the local theatre every week. There is no reason to expect that children should have any such "rights" in these areas either. What I have to say here will apply only to *bona fide* rights, and to all of them. I am making this suggestion in all seriousness, and with the full realization that many people will find it crazy, dangerous, or otherwise abhorrent.

To make the case for equal rights for children, I shall first (Chapter I) have to explain the development of the idea of child-protection in some detail. Child-protection has been a useful guide for the development of many of our institutions and policies concerning children over the years. One does not need to minimize its accomplishments to see its weaknesses in the area of respect for children. The remedy for these weaknesses will not be found in larger doses of child protection. A fresh response to our relationships with children is in order, and I think it is to be found in the notion of equal rights for children.

Accordingly, I want to explain the role of the concept of rights in the movement to change our treatment of children (Chapter II). Rights structure some of our social relationships by entitling people who have them to make certain demands— legal, moral, or both—on others. There are basically three grounds for making these demands: We might defend children's rights as human rights (Chapter III), as a matter of social justice (Chapters IV-VII), or because our society would be better off with such rights than it would be without them (Chapters VIII-X). The line of defense which is most appropriate will depend in part on the right, in part on the society, and in part on the tactics of the movement for social change.

At the present, considerations of social justice seem most compelling to me for most rights, and I shall argue for an end to the double standard of rights primarily on those grounds (Chapter IV). Social justice, in one of its basic dimensions, requires that people in similar circumstances be treated similarly and that those in different circumstances be treated differently. We may further assume that people should be treated equally until and unless they can be shown to be unequal.[1] To do otherwise is to show favoritism, to be unfair, or to be arbitrary. Of course, where circumstances are not similar, differences in treatment are quite appropriate. So the main question for the children's rights movement comes to this: Are children relevantly similar to adults or not with respect to having rights? If they are, the double standard is unjust; if not, it is not.

The key to this question is the concept of *capacities*. These are the things which children are most often said to lack and which are most often thought to be necessary for the meaningful exercise of at least some rights. It is my contention that the difference in capacities between some adults and some children is not relevant when it comes to handing out rights (Chapter V). It is not relevant because capacities may be *borrowed*. That is, people who do not have them may be able to engage those who do in order to exercise certain rights. As long as we can designate *agents* with the relevant capacities to serve those children who wish to exercise their rights, social justice will require that we do so. There are bound to be difficulties with the idea of putting the capacities of agents at the disposal of children. Some of these will be theoretical and some will be practical. I shall deal with as many of them as I can think of (Chapters V-VI), and try to assess the impact of this proposal on family life as we know it (Chapter VII).

In the last part of the book, I look more closely at three specific kinds of rights in order to guage the impact of extending them to children. Chapter VIII examines the rights of political participation; Chapter IX, the rights of procedural due process of law in court; and Chapter X, the rights of privacy. While a case can be made for extending all of these rights to children on the basis of social justice, it seems to me that our society would also be better off if we abolished the double standard in these areas. However, my aim here is not simply to strengthen the case for equal rights for children. I also want to suggest some of the ways in which the more theoretical aspects of my discussion can be brought to bear on questions of social policy. I am confident that many people who work with children and who care for them believe that children do deserve to have equal rights in our society. If anything is more difficult than believing this in the face of the child-protection ideal, it is putting it into practice where "supervision" has been the dominant form of relating to children. By elaborating the benefits of agents rather than supervisors for some rights, I hope to provide a model which others may use to work on rights more closely related to their own areas of concern. The transition from theory to social policy is not always easy to see, but it is crucial if we plan to do more than just talk about children's rights.

Equal Rights
For
Children

CHAPTER I

Child Protection; Children's Rights

Children are surely the most vulnerable and powerless people in our society. Although this is in some sense not terribly controversial, we have great difficulty coming to grips with its full meaning. We regularly obscure, minimize, ignore, and even deny this fact. We do so by reminding ourselves that children are loved by adults, cared for, protected, treated specially, guided, prized and praised. While this is all more or less true for many, perhaps most, children most of the time, it speaks not at all to vulnerability and powerlessness. For children are loved and reared as adults see fit; they are literally at the mercy of adults. (Mercy, after all, is given from love, not obligation.) No matter how much adults do for children—no matter how much kindness and good will we express—what is done is done on adult terms. Children may not *demand* anything of us. At most other adults (or the state) may require this or that *for* a child, but children may only request; they may not insist.

The essential powerlessness of children is nowhere more apparent than in the matter of child abuse. Most people see the helplessness of children most clearly and react most strongly when adults—parents especially—are violent toward children or sexually assault them. This has been particularly apparent in official and public reaction to recent reports of child abuse.

In Massachusetts, for example, three recent, widely-reported cases in which children died at the hands of their parents have severely shaken the Public Welfare bureaucracy and the general populace. Although these cases were quite grotesque, and no doubt not typical, examples of child abuse, they nevertheless have helped people to see the larger dimensions of the problem.

Child abuse became front page news in Boston with the discovery of the death of two-year-old Jennifer Gallison. Jennifer, according to her mother's testimony, had apparently died of a severe blow on the head. Her father allegedly dismembered her body and left it for rubbish collection in a plastic trash bag. At the time of her death, her parents were under investigation for the abuse of their four-year-old son, Edward, as well. People's initial shock focused on the grizzly disposal of Jennifer's body and the callousness of the attacks on both children. But these horrors gave way to another. These children were not only defenseless, they were invisible. Their abuse was not an isolated act which quickly came to light; it went on for a long time and was not really comprehended by the social workers involved with the Gallison family. Indeed *Minor Affairs* reports: "An unbelievable series of errors was climaxed by a worker's report that Jennifer Gallison was eating and sleeping well and staying healthy, which turned out to have been made two and a half months after Jennifer died."[1] Not only were these children utterly vulnerable, they were ultimately unprotected.

Not long after the Gallison case, the body of Elizabeth Nassar (five months old) was found in a plastic bag awaiting rubbish collection. Her parents claimed that she had suffocated. Further investigation into this case revealed serious neglect of another daughter and death of a son. The parents were convicted of neglect of two girls; manslaughter charges on the son's death were dropped for insufficient evidence.

Later in the year child abuse made headlines again with the death of eleven-year-old Dianne DeVanna. She died of a blood clot on the brain which was apparently caused by blows to the head. Dianne was reportedly beaten daily for two weeks and continuously for eight hours before she died. Her father and his wife were charged with murder. This case, too, revealed more than the defenselessness of children against adult rage. Dianne had been a ward of the state from 1976 (when her father remarried) until 1978. In August of 1978 she was returned to her father's custody—with the approval of the Welfare Department, the staff of a child care center where she had lived, and a county judge. Here, too, it is clear that there are no guarantees that the state can really protect children who are liable to be abused.

What is to be learned from these horrors? First, I suppose, that we may not rely on "parental instinct" to protect children from harm. When we call something an instinct we mean it is ingrained in all parents and it will come through in the end. But if some parents don't have this deep sense of protection and care for their offspring, or if these feelings and impulses break down under stress, then the point of the label "instinct" is lost. The question then becomes who has it and who doesn't—and we'd better find out if our aim is to prevent child abuse. The very existence of parents who have brutalized their children shows that we would be kidding ourselves if we thought that nature has provided for this problem.

A second lesson brought home by these cases is that child abuse is *much* more widespread than we would like to admit. As stories of abused children became public knowledge, people demanded to know why these abusive parents were not detected before their children were dead. Why was there no early warning and intervention? Such questions, coupled with new and stronger abuse reporting laws, lead to closer looks and more discoveries. Case workers are now being trained to find and deal with child abuse; they report that they do not have far to look. In fact the magnitude of the problem is steadily being revised upward as researchers investigate more carefully. A recent report estimated that *two million* American children are abused each year. (The investigator, himself, regarded this figure as low.)[2] Two million people is roughly the population of Philadelphia.

A third lesson is that child abuse can no longer be treated as merely a psychological problem. Abusive parents have psychological problems to be sure. But it is not enough to say that they are unbalanced, abnormal, weak of will, irresponsible or whatever. Even if this is all true, the fact remains that there are no *structures* in the family, the community or the larger society to put the brakes on troubled adults. The fact that there are two million abused children does not point to a few deviants who slipped through the cracks. It shows that our social institutions do not have adequate structures or mechanisms to keep potential abusers in check or make them change their ways.

This is a very important point, and its full importance is not easy to grasp. If psychological help for abusive parents is not an adequate response to the problem, then we must be ready to accept the idea that dealing with child abuse will mean changing the structures of all relationships between adults and children— not merely the bad ones. If we can not say in advance which adults are likely to abuse children and which are not, then we can not reduce child abuse by treating parental problems case by case. We would be too late—and probably do too little as well. To treat the problem seriously, then, we would have to find a way to build checks against child abuse into all our relationships with children. In other words, child abuse would no longer be somebody else's problem; its solution would affect us all.

The idea here is like a safety valve or a back-up system. A driver may never need to use an emergency brake on the road and a hospital may never use its auxiliary power generators, but they are integral parts of their respective systems. They are built in from the beginning, not added as a need arises. They must be ready for use anytime and not merely in risky situations.

In human relationships the safety valve is integrated into the structure in two parts: standards of behavior and accountability for actions. Some relationships are rather flexible and ill-defined. People could treat one another in a whole variety of ways and not be out of line. Parents presently relate to children in this open manner. They may be formal or casual, strict or permissive, models or companions, intimate or distant, and so on. All of these styles and ranges are acceptable ways of parenting, and there is no clear sense of when the relationship has been violated.

Similarly, parents are not generally held accountable for their relationships with their children. Parenting is still *largely* a private matter. If an adult does not wish to discuss it, it is not discussed. There are exceptions, of course, in the cases of demonstrated abuse or neglect when a court is involved, and in cases of public assistance to families with children. But by and large, parents answer to nobody for the relationship they create with their children. In short, parent-child relationships are too indefinite to have a safety valve built into them which would be an adequate brake on child abuse. In order to face up to the vulnerability and powerlessness of children, then, we must reconsider our relationships to them.

The dominant thrust of concern for the treatment of children in contemporary America has been for more "care taking." In response to a perceived need for more structure in adult-child relationships, those with the caretaker outlook have sought new ways to protect children from real and potential abuses. Caretakers have been responsible for institutionalizing compulsory education, limitations on child labor, laws prohibiting child abuse and neglect, aid to families with dependent children, school lunch programs, infant health programs, some public support for day care, and so on.

The caretaker conception of child protection has been around for quite some time. Indeed, it was clearly and eloquently expressed by John Locke in the *Second Treatise of Government* (1691). There he characterizes the relationship between parent and child as follows:

Adam was created a perfect man, his body and mind in full possession of their strength and reason, and so was capable from the first instant of his being to provide for his own support and preservation and govern his actions according to the dictates of the law of reason which God had implanted in him. From him the world is peopled with his descendants who are all born infants, weak and helpless, without knowledge or understanding; but to supply the defects of this imperfect state till the improvement of growth and age has removed them, Adam and Eve, and after them all parents, were by the law of nature "under an obligation to preserve, nourish, and educate the children" they had begotten; not as their own workmanship, but the workmanship of their own Maker, the Almighty, to whom they were to be accountable for them.[3]

This passage contains most of the important elements of what we are calling the caretaker conception of child protection.

Children are not merely property. Notice first that the children belong to God. In Locke's view, a view commonly held in the seventeenth century, the fruits of a person's labor were that person's private property. Under the circumstances, it would be quite reasonable to think of one's children as one's property. This is specifically rejected by making children God's property. Parents are to take care of children for God. This is part of the moral and spiritual function of the modern family. The child must be raised to live the sort of life which is pleasing to God. Locke says this is a life in accordance with the "dictates of the law of reason."

Children have their own futures. As God's property, the child has a life of his or her own, for God does not regard us as his commodities. In the first place, I suppose, He has no need of commodities. But more to the point, seventeenth century spirituality saw God's work as the creation of an orderly, well-governed universe in which each independent part was in harmony with all the others. God's children, then, were destined to take their place in the moral and social order as individuals and not merely in service to some larger unit (the family). This gave them a present status as potential independent beings. But one cannot over-stress that the independence was potential.

Children lack human capacities, but not humanity. "Children are born weak and helpless, without knowledge and understanding." In short, they do not yet have what is required to be a being pleasing to God. They do not have the reason which would enable them to live under the law of reason. They are in need of care. Locke says they are born to a state of equality, but not in a state of equality. The point to notice here is that things can turn out well or badly. There are no guarantees that the weak infant will become the reasoning adult. Parents must take steps to see that the "improvement of growth and age" actually come about.

The child's weakness is a source of parental authority which in turn is a source of parental obligation. As a result, parents are under an obligation to "preserve, nourish, and educate" their children. This is not a choice they have. It comes with the job of being a caretaker. The obligation is not to the child, but to God. Therefore, the child may not refuse the services or release them from their obligation. So while the protection of the child is for the child's own good, its principal justification is that God has an interest in order and social harmony. This brings us to the last main element of the caretaker ideology.

Parents can know and do what is best for children. The best interests of the child, the parent, and of the society at large are perceived to be in harmony. No doubt, this was easier to believe when people thought that God orchestrated the world order, but the assumption remains a part of the beliefs about child protection. It is in the interest of the child to become a well-developed adult; it is the interest of society to have a new generation of well-developed adults; and it is in the interest of the parents to bring their caretaking obligations to a satisfactory end and to give a good account of themselves. Thus, there are, in theory, no built-in conflicts in childrearing. Should a parent prove to do a poor job of caretaking, it is never explained by a conflict of interests. Rather, the parent is regarded as unfit: unable to pursue the child's interests, and hence unable to pursue his or her own interests either.

Although the caretaker ideology was clearly articulated by Locke almost three hundred years ago, its acceptance has been quite gradual. The view that Providence still has more to do with a child's life than parental effort does did not disappear easily. Indeed, it is still believed in some quarters today. So the battle for a child's right to protection has been the battle to bring those inclined to leave events to God or the Seasons to recognize and assume their powers over their children's lives. This, I think, helps to account for the moralistic and missionary tone of most child care manuals before Dr. Spock's. They are aimed at parents who are not only presumed to want information, but who are assumed to be unaware of the seriousness of childrearing.

The caretaker approach to children's vulnerability is pretty clearly to structure more responsibility into the parental role. Where parents do not, cannot or will not assume that responsibility, the state does so (acting in their place as parent). In short, there is no effort to diminish the vulnerability and powerlessness of children, but only to buffer them from the potential consequences of their condition. When things get worse for children, caretakers respond with larger doses of protection.

The caretaker conception of how to relate to children has come under severe attack in the last few years. The problem is that in the course of protecting children we have stunted the fullness of our relationship to them and have slighted them as people. Consider the remarks of three well-known advocates for American youth:

I wish to pose a question that has preoccupied me for the past couple of years: Do we Americans *really* like children?
After considerable reflection, I suggest that the answer is: Yes, *if* our sentiments are to be taken as evidence. Yes, we do like children, and even love them—if the test is in the values we profess and in the myths we cherish, celebrate, and pass on from generation to generation. However, I am prepared to assert that in spite of our tender sentiments, we do *not* really like children. We do not as a nation really love them in practice, and I am sure that all of you will agree that what we do must finally provide the evidence that answers the question.[4]

Kenneth Keniston

Our world is not a good place for children. Every institution in our society severely discriminates against them. We all come to feel that it is either natural or necessary to cooperate in that discrimination. Unconsciously, we carry out the will of a society which holds a limited and demeaned view of children and which refuses to recognize their right to full humanity.[5]

Richard Farson

For a long time it never occurred to me to question [modern childhood]. Only in recent years did I begin to wonder whether there might be other or better ways for young people to live. By now I have come to feel that the fact of being a "child," of being seen by older people as a mixture of expansive nuisance, slave, and super-pet, does most young people more harm than good.[6]

John Holt

These criticisms are grounded in an alternative to the care-taker conception of the treatment of children. We are invited to consider not only the sad stories but also the lot of the typical child. If some children are brutalized, it is partly because all children are demeaned or at least not respected. Improvement for the worst off can not be separated from improvement for the rest. The new child advocates are no longer saying that we do not do enough for our children; they are saying that we are doing the wrong things. Richard Farson divides child advocates into two groups: "On the one hand there are those who are interested in protecting children, and on the other those who are interested in protecting children's rights."[7] He regards the first group as "paternalistic," and places himself in the second, which is more interested in liberation than protection. What it would mean to liberate children is, of course, a long story. But the point here is that it is also a new story. It marks a departure from the aims of more traditional child advocates. The new advocates tend to think of children more as an oppressed minority than as a collection of small and helpless beings, some of whom are, sadly, ill-treated.

This new perspective has wider implications. The traditional concerns of those who want to protect children have been to protect them against *abusers*. The very idea of an "abuser" suggests that there is a standard of normal treatment which is perfectly acceptable and beyond criticism. As a rule, children are properly treated. But in some circumstances, be they poverty, ignorance, irresponsibility, immorality, or callous indifference, parents or caretakers fail to live up to the standard. Child protectors want to punish abusers or help them to change, but in either case their concern is with this socially deviant group which everyone hopes is not too large. As painful as it is to think of children being mistreated, it is somewhat comforting to believe that others are responsible. On the caretaker conception, it is difficult to make the transition which helps us to see how our normal relations with children contribute to child abuse.

The new child advocates on the other hand, see the standard, normal, socially acceptable treatment of children as part of the problem. It is the very institution of American childhood which they are attacking. In other words, they are saying that our fundamental ways of relating to children are inadequate, and that we must restructure them. This is a criticism which none of us may escape. We are denied our indignation at the failures of others; we may take no comfort in our own good intentions or kindly feelings toward children. As adults in a society which oppresses children, we are part of the problem.

As a society we have come to understand that there is not only personal bigotry, but institutional racism; not only male chauvinism, but economic and social discrimination against women. We are now being asked to acknowledge that there is not only child abuse, but systematic mistreatment of children.

The comparison is harsh and likely to be misunderstood. It is important not to take this as merely an occasion to spread a little blame or to make people feel guilty for their social institutions. If our aim is social change, the real point of comparing children to black people and women is to give "movement status" to the various efforts to change and improve children's lives.

People who are concerned with the status of children in our society may, as a practical matter, have very little to do with one another. Some are interested in juvenile delinquency and court reform; others in the quality of education; still others in children's health care, day care services, adoption and foster care, political participation, sexual abuse, censorship, and so on. It is hard for people who work on a single issue—which is often local—to find support in the efforts of people in other places working on very different issues. But when child advocates begin to recognize their mutual interests and see the common threads which run through their various efforts, patterns begin to emerge. What may once have seemed like a very special problem becomes one more version of a same old story. At least this is the expectation on the part of those who think of children as an oppressed minority. Once we adopt the proper vantage point, things will fall into place. And along with a new understanding, we can look for closer ties among child advocates which will mean more effective efforts to bring about desired changes in all areas of our treatment of children.

The common threads which unite advocates of a new relationship with children are, first, a deep dissatisfaction with the basic assumptions of the caretaker outlook, and second, a conviction that children must be treated more like adults in certain respects.

Caretakers tend to treat children's rights exclusively in terms of protection. Children's rights advocates, however, see at least three assumptions which the child protectionists make which are regarded as suspect. The first of these is that adults are able to perceive what is in a child's best interest. When we are dealing with other adults, we tend to acknowledge that each individual is the best judge of her or his own best interests. This, of course, is not always true. Some people are hopeless when it comes to seeing their own best interest. They always manage to do the thing which puts them at the greatest disadvantage or makes them most unhappy. But this is the exception; and even for them it is easier to say what is not in their best interest than to say what is. It is very hard to be confident about how another person perceives a situation, and to be sure that you have taken all the factors which are important to them into account. So we tend to take their word for it when they say that something is or is not in their interest. What we lack in knowledge to make those judgments, they compensate for in intuitions about themselves.

We do not make similar concessions to children, however. They are not presumed to have a sufficiently developed set of intuitions about themselves, or a sufficient awareness of what is important to them to make even roughly accurate judgments about their own self-interest. Now while this may be true, and certainly is true for many children, it is not true for all children. But what is more to the point is that a child's ignorance of her or his own self-interest does not improve the adult's knowledge of that child's best interest. The adult is in the same position with respect to the child that he or she is with respect to any other person. All of the difficulties about making a judgment for another remain. While it is not obvious what one should do in this situation, it is at least clear that the child protectionists have assumed that they have a kind of knowledge which it is doubtful that they really do have. And this assumption itself is a potential source of the disintegration of the quality of child care.

The second problem with the caretaker ideology is that it obscures the possibility of a conflict of interest between child and adult. This is partly a consequence of the first point. If the child is disregarded as a judge of her or his own best interest, then expressions of conflict coming from the child will not be taken seriously. Furthermore, the very adults who are engaged in the conflict are usually the adults who determine what the child's best interest is. And it is obviously in *their* interest to deny the conflict. But this is only part of the problem with the assumption of social harmony among adults and children.

What makes the assumption of a community of interest

among children and their caretaking adults plausible in the first place is the belief that the interests of both are tied to the interest of a larger unit, for example, the family, which they share in common. Thus, if John Jones acts in his best interest as a father, he is acting in the best interest of all the other family members. If John Jones were only a father, there would be no problem here other than trying to decide what actually is in the best interest of the family. However, John Jones has other social attachments. He is an employee, an organization member, a neighbor, a friend, and so on. In each of these capacities, he has interests—and these interests do not always coincide with his interests as father. Likewise, his children have other social attachments: student, organization member, neighbor, friend. They too have interests which may not coincide with their interests as family members. In complex societies where one's family is not the only or sometimes even the most important group to which one belongs, it is not very plausible to assume that the interests of adults and children will always be in harmony. Again, it is the refusal to recognize these potential conflicts and to think about how to deal with them which children's rights advocates perceive as a source of poor quality child care inherent in the child protection ideology.

The third assumption which the new children's rights advocates challenge is the assumption that the quality of care can be improved by passing control over children from adult to adult. In this way, the question of whether the control over the child is itself a problem never arises. Adults as a general rule object to being treated paternalistically—that is, in the ways that parents treat their children. There are instances in which we accept a measure of paternalism, to be sure. Motorcyclists are required to wear helmets for their own protection. But for the most part, we only accept this in cases of serious social concern, or as a last resort. The reason for this is that paternalism tends to undermine one's sense of dignity. The presumption is that the person who is the object of control cannot be reasoned with—cannot be brought to see his or her best interest. And while we agreed that this sometimes happens, to make a regular presumption of it is to deny a person all of the opportunities by which one's dignity is established. Without being able to take control over one's actions, one cannot take credit for them. Here, too, children's rights advocates find the ideology of child protection lacking.

I have outlined these criticisms not so much to establish the deficiencies of child protection as to explain the context in which child advocates are now demanding equal rights for children. The debate over the accuracy of the assumptions still lies before us. And it is clear that we will have to evaluate the virtues and defects of protection as they arise in the discussion of particular rights. For it is fairly specific rights which the child advocates have in mind. Two of the writers who have been clearest about this are Richard Farson and John Holt. Farson makes self-determination the basic right: "Children should have the right to decide matters that effect them most directly." Whatever is needed to make this possible—to reduce the control that adults have over the lives of children—Farson would specify as a child's right. Holt takes the position that children should have "the right to do, in general, what any adult may legally do." Since adults are presumed to be self-determining in this society, this way of putting it comes to pretty much the same thing.

What child advocates want is an end of legal and social discrimination against children in most areas of life. The extent of the program is best captured in one of the numerous bills of rights which have been proposed for children. The rights enumerated by Farson in *Birthrights* typify the sorts of things that the advocates have in mind:

1. The Right to Self-Determination. Children should have the right to decide matters that affect them most directly.
2. The Right to Alternate Home Environments. Self-determining children should be able to choose from among a variety of arrangements: residences operated by children, child-exchange programs, twenty-four hour child-care centers, and various kinds of schools and employment opportunities.
3. The Right to Responsive Design. Society must accommodate itself to children's size and to their need for safe space.
4. The Right to Information. A child must have the right to all information ordinarily available to adults—including, and perhaps especially, information that makes adults uncomfortable.

5. The Right to Educate Oneself. Children should be free to design their own education, choosing from among many options the kinds of learning experiences they want, including the option not to attend any kind of school.

6. The Right to Freedom from Physical Punishment. Children should live free of physical threat from those who are larger and more powerful than they.

7. The Right to Sexual Freedom. Children should have the right to conduct their sexual lives with no more restriction than adults.

8. The Right to Economic Power. Children should have the right to work, to acquire and manage money, to receive equal pay for equal work, to choose trade apprenticeship as an alternative to school, to gain promotion to leadership positions, to own property, to develop a credit record, to enter into binding contracts, to engage in enterprise, to obtain guaranteed support apart from the family, to achieve financial independence.

9. The Right to Justice. Children must have the guarantee of a fair trial with due process of law, an advocate to protect their rights against parents as well as the system, and a uniform standard of detention.[8]

There is no denying that these are radical proposals which would have far-reaching consequences for American society. There is an overwhelming temptation to plunge into the list and try to imagine what life would be like if children had such rights. This temptation is only a little less powerful than the temptation to reject these suggestions out of hand as the product of a hopeless idealist. I think for the present we should resist both of these temptations, and ask instead what it means to demand these things for children as *rights*. That is, we need to know something about what rights are before we can decide whether or not children should have them.

CHAPTER II

Why Rights?

In order to have a clearer understanding of what it means to advocate *children's* rights, then, we should shift our emphasis to an examination of children's *rights*. In other words, what does it mean to talk about the treatment of children in the language of rights? When we say that someone has a right to something, we are saying that they are entitled to it, or that they have a valid claim on it. These are ways of defining our relations to one another in society. In certain matters we must stand aside, or perhaps see to it that others receive what they are entitled to. Not all social relationships are like this, of course. A person may have a right to vote or to a trial by jury. But we surely do not have a right to a birthday present from our mothers. The difference is in the entitlement. We reserve talk about rights for serious matters where we wish to make strong statements about the treatment of others. So to say that children should have certain rights which they do not have now is to say more than that we are unhappy about the way children are being treated. We are talking about a large-scale serious effort to restructure relationships with children in our society. To have a better sense of what this means, it is helpful to remind ourselves of other groups which have raised the issue of their treatment in terms of rights.

The concept of "rights" is most commonly used in the context of fairly specific social movements: the Civil Rights Movement, the women's movement, the student movement, and a variety of others for the rights of senior citizens, gays, and prisoners, to name the most notable. In each of these instances people with common goals have acted, and are acting, to have particular kinds of treatment recognized in custom and in law. The Civil Rights Movement sought an end to segregation of black people, housing and job discrimination against them, and an end to their exclusion from the political process. Equal treatment and full participation in this society is demanded as a matter of right. The women's movement is focused around a variety of themes of male dominance with an end to economic discrimination as its core. Equal pay for equal work, and equal access to jobs are demanded as a matter of right. Students have demanded an end to arbitrary regulations of their conduct and a recognized role in the selection of curriculum. Senior citizens are demanding an end to mandatory retirement; gays are demanding an end to job discrimination and harassment; prisoners are demanding an end to harsh and arbitrary treatment. Although the specific issues raised by each of these groups are much more complicated than I have just suggested, the general point about the concept of rights emerges quite clearly: groups raise the issue of rights, in the context of perceived discrimination which is practiced or at least tolerated, by the larger society. The right is demanded as a means toward ending the discrimination; its establishment implies a restructuring of social relationships.

In later chapters, we will see how this works in some detail with specific rights. For example, political rights, including the right to vote, are important partly for their own sake, since their denial marks second-class status. But these rights are also important because they help to open the political process (to some extent) as another arena in which to combat discrimination. The absence of rights before the law, especially in juvenile court procedures, is also a source of great discretion, which in turn causes discrimination against youth. Likewise, the lack of privacy rights for children makes those children vulnerable to unregulated adult control. An established right to privacy is another tool for establishing decent relationships among adults and children. The various ways in which these particular rights can shape those relationships need to be probed fairly thoroughly, but we must first lay the groundwork for treating these questions as "rights" issues.

Calling for children's rights will not, by itself, change things very much. There is little reason to believe that official recognition of rights—even writing them into law—will end discrimination. There is a great difference between establishing a right and enforcing one. Enforcement of rights is something that occurs on a personal level. A particular landlord is required to rent to a particular black tenant. A particular employer is required to raise the salary of a particular female employee. A particular principal is required to allow a particular student to wear an armband to school. When these rights are enforced, these instances of discrimination are ended. When we speak of establishing rights, we are talking about changes in the kind of treatment that entire groups of people are to receive. Rights movements set out to change the standards of acceptable practice in specific situations. They deal with institutional discrimination rather than with personal prejudice. This is an important point for understanding the demand for children's rights. Advocates are not simply saying that this child or that child has been ill-treated, abused, or discriminated against. It is not a question of protecting some child against the occasional uncaring or prejudiced adult. The standards of treatment themselves are being called into question. Even if all children were treated strictly according to the book, children's rights advocates would still insist that the book be rewritten. Once new standards of relating to children are established, then we deal with personal instances of discrimination through the enforcement of rights.

Another major point to notice about associating children's treatment with other rights movements is that a level of militancy is injected into the issue. "Rights" is a militant concept to the extent that it is used as part of the ideology in a campaign for social change. In our society people generally recognize that it is bad to have your rights denied, and that something should be done about it. Having you rights denied is not merely bad in the way that not receiving a birthday present from your mother might be. In that case you would have our sympathy, but little more. That is not the sort of ill-treatment that motivates others to action. In order to involve others in cases of mistreatment, it is important to show that a denial of right is involved. To say that relations with children could be better does not have the urgency that goes with saying that their rights are being denied. As a tactical matter in movements for social change, a group is in a stronger position if it can make its case in terms of rights. People who are engaged in serious efforts to bring about social change tend to use the concept of rights in a militant way: to discredit the opposition, to bring them around, to win support from neutral parties, and to gain some formal recognition of the desired changes.

The suitability of the concept of rights as a vehicle for social change is largely dependent on our sense of what it means to be entitled to do or have something. As "entitlements," rights are most easily understood in contrast to the treatment of others on the basis of permission, privilege, granting favors, and allowing. For example, I do not have a right to fish on a privately owned lake; I must asked permission. Local residents may have the privilege of gathering firewood in the town forest, although others are prohibited from doing so. The privilege may be revoked if the town leaders feel that wood gathering is creating a problem. My neighbor offers me the use of his ladder as a favor. If I need it again, I may not simply take it—nor should I expect to. He may let me use it with great regularity, but each time he does so as a favor; I may not presume to have any special claim on the ladder's use. Again, I may be allowed to pick blueberries in a state forest—the state has no regulation against doing so. While it is true that I need not ask the forest ranger's permission, it is also true that the state could pass a regulation prohibiting berry picking at any time. In each of these cases, the fact that I have had or done something in the past does not establish a precedent for the future. My relationships with the town, my neighbor and the state are ones which leave them in control of the respective situations.

In contrast to these situations is the situation in which I am entitled to do or have something. My action is not dependent upon the discretion of others. It has been decided in advance— by law or through custom—that I may engage in certain activities or have certain things without regard for the wishes, desires, or approval of others. I need not ask anyone in order to do what

I am entitled to do; nor are their objections to my doing it relevant. When a person is entitled in this way, we say she or he has a right to something.

When someone has a right in this sense of the term, others are thereby obligated to act in particular ways. Exactly what their obligations are will, of course, depend on the particular right in question, but in general there are two sorts of obligation. First there are obligations of non-interference: *If a person has a right to something, then everyone else has an obligation not to interfere with that person's having or doing that thing.* These obligations are very general and apply to literally everyone else in the world. For most people most of the time, this obligation is irrelevant: they are in no position to interfere in the first place. But the point is that if they should find themselves in such a position, they may not interfere. It is expressed this way to cover all contingencies. For some rights, obligations of non-interference are sufficient. As long as others are prohibited from interfering, a person has the particular right. Insofar as it does not require others to actually provide a forum, the right to free speech is of this type. But other rights require us to do more than stand aside. They may provide obligations of performance: *If a person has a right to something, then someone has an obligation to help that person have or do that thing.* These obligations are quite specific: they apply to particular persons and define particular kinds of help. Which persons and what help will depend upon who has the right and what right it is, so this cannot be decided in advance. It is decided when rights which carry obligations of performance are created and defined. Many consumer protection rights are of this type. For example, the right to renege on a contract for up to three days after signing it obligates the other party to return any money you may have paid for goods or services. A problem about rights in general—and children's rights in particular—is how to decide which create obligations of non-interference alone, and which create obligations of performance. But this problem will have to be set aside until we have considered the concept of a child's agent and applied it to particular examples.

When a person has a right, then, it limits the discretion with which others may act toward her or him in specific areas. There are two main consequences of this sort of relationship which are especially important for children's rights issues. A loss of discretion over others means a loss of control over the conduct of their lives, and it also means relating to them in a less informal and more prescribed way. We need to understand this in order to see why it is that some people see the very idea of rights for children (any rights at all) as a threat to family relationships as we know them.

If rights are to be meaningful, they must be expressed precisely enough to spell out what others must or must not do. Thus, others may be explicitly required to stand aside from or aid in activities which they happen to disapprove of. And even where they do not specifically disapprove of a given activity, there is always the potential for finding themselves in that position. For rights are usually expressed in ways which give their holders a range of options, any one of which he or she is entitled to pursue. Others may approve of the option which is in fact chosen, but realize that they would be in no position to object had the holder of the right decided differently. This is what is usually on the minds of parents who would gladly extend as privileges the same things which are being demanded as rights.

Many parents want to see their children make their own decisions—as long as those decisions are "responsible." The child is allowed to make decisions as long as the privilege is not abused. What counts as an abuse is, of course, left to the discretion of the parents. So the child may decide when to study, when to work, when to socialize, where to go, and who to have as friends. As long as this works out to the satisfaction of everyone concerned, the child has a measure of freedom. What the child does not have is a right to regulate his or her activity in this sphere. If the parents disapprove of the decisions which are actually made, they may—at their discretion—limit the range of options or remove it entirely. The parents are justified in revoking a privilege in a way that they would not be justified in interfering with an entitlement. The difference has to do with control and where it ultimately resides—with the child or with the parent. In the contemporary American family, control clearly resides in the parents (or in the state should it become involved in family matters). Talk about children's *rights* threatens to change this—and with it traditional patterns of family relationships.

The shift of control over children's activities is not the only impact that the restriction of parental discretion would have on the family. There is another more subtle, but equally momentous, consequence. Discretion thrives on vagueness. When rights are expressed in vague terms—like a right to security, or happiness, or reasonable consideration—others are left with the discretion to interpret these terms as they see fit. The extent of leeway they retain over interpretation is equivalent to the amount of control they maintain over what they must or must not do. If they have too much leeway in crucial respects, the "right" in question is hardly more than a privilege. Consequently, rights should be expressed specifically enough to insure that their holders cannot be thwarted through interpretation from those things that the right was designed to allow them to do. It is, I suppose, impossible to eliminate discretion entirely. One cannot anticipate every situation and enumerate it in the expression of the right. And discretion in any areas which would not subvert the intent of the right may be safely ignored. But there is a drafting problem about rights, and in general, it is better to be overly specific than overly vague—especially where it is likely that others will try to use their discretion to regain a measure of control. The difficulty that this raises here is that it will tend to formalize some aspects of family relationships. Members of a family will sometimes have to behave toward one another in accordance with fixed rules. Not in all aspects of family life, to be sure, but in some important ones. The fear is that this formality will hinder the development of "natural" (that is, close and caring) relationships among family members. Formality, it is said, puts an emotional distance between people and encourages them to ritualize their responses toward one another. Closeness results from informality—the absence of rules or the possibility of setting them aside. If this is really so, then the introduction of children's rights would turn the family into just another living arrangement.

The other major worry that people have about the effect of children's rights on the family is less a consequence of the loss of parental discretion than of the official status of the right.

When one has a right, one is not only entitled, but the entitlement has a status in custom or law. What that means as a practical matter is that one may appeal to others for support if one's rights are being denied. In effect the child may call upon an outsider—a relative, a friend, a stranger, or even the law— to enforce a right. That is not only embarrassing, but it also undermines the basis of the traditional conception of the difference between our relations to family and to others. The family is usually viewed as the sanctuary of privacy in an otherwise public world. There are, to be sure, exceptions when the state may intrude—but they are exceptions. Official recognition of children's rights would pave the way for more intrusion: by the state and by others. And this would surely undermine our sense of what is private and what is public business.

I have been trying to suggest ways in which the language of rights itself will shape the various proposals for changes in the ways we treat children. For it is important to realize that it is not simply the proposals themselves—their content—which children's rights advocates demand. Children are said to have a *right* to these things—an entitlement, as we have been using the term. This way of thinking about children will have a fairly substantial social impact over and above the effects of any detailed changes in the way we relate to them.

By now it should be fairly clear what is at stake in the call for children's rights. What remains to be explored here are the ways in which this call is made. That is, we need a sense of the strategy involved in a movement to establish rights where they have not previously been recognized. There are roughly three ways that the concept of rights can be used in campaigns for social change. A group can claim that it is being denied rights which it already has but which the larger society wrongly refused to recognize. These are usually characterized as human rights or natural rights. Second, the group can claim that rights which are recognized for others in the society should be extended to it as well, on the grounds that there are no significant differences between them and the others. This is the demand for social justice. Finally, the group can claim that a progressive society should seek to establish new rights for its members, on the grounds that the society will be better off if it does so. Here the claim to rights is based on the anticipation of social benefits. Because of the militant nature of many rights campaigns, the line of argument which is used to establish any particular right is often arrived at as a tactical decision. The decision is made on the basis of which argument is likely to be most successful. The first claim probably has a strategic edge in this regard because it assumes an on-going injury to human dignity. But whether it applies accurately to any given right and the society in question can only be determined by looking at particular cases. When we come to examine in more detail rights which are recommended for children, we will need to see how one—or more—of these claims are appropriate for each right.

Rights which everyone is said to have whether they are acknowledged by others or not are usually called human rights or natural rights. People are supposed to have human rights simply because they are members of the species. As species members, they have the capacity to be dignified, or to reason or to make choices, or to be reflective, or to feel pain, and so on. Because of these features—whichever is stressed—which all humans share, some people claim that we have certain rights which preserve and protect them as distinctively human features. Natural rights are explained in a similar way, except that the features referred to are not simply characteristics of human beings, but characteristics of basic social relationships. That is, relationships which people would have to have in any and every society—no matter how different societies are in the detail of their customs. Examples of such relationships are "reciprocity" (you scratch my back, and I'll scratch yours) and certain biological relationships such as that between parent and child. In order to maintain such relationships, it is said, they must be governed by certain rights.

Now obviously, if it were true that a person had a human or natural right to something, then the fact that the rest of society did not acknowledge the right could not seriously be used to discount the claim. Indeed the society would be shown to be out of line with humanitarian or basic social practices—and in need of prompt restructuring. Furthermore, the appeal for support to establish the right can be directed to those outside the society as well. The level of appeal is so basic that the question of treating people differently in different cultures does not arise. Supporters of human or natural rights are not embarrassed by cultural diversity. The United Nations Universal Declaration of Human Rights is supposed to apply to everyone in the world. In this respect the appeal to human or natural rights is a powerful ideological tool.

Nevertheless, there are pitfalls for this strategy. When the discrimination one wishes to end is a very specific kind, or is created by the existence of sophisticated technology, it is quite difficult to make the link between the particular right and general features of humanity or society. Suppose that people are arguing for the right to state-financed medical care. Could we really convince others that Medicare is the logical outcome of the fact that people are rational, able to make choices, reflective, or live in reciprocal relationships? We might convince them that we had a right to "health" which is, no doubt, necessary for a full and active human social life. But health is one thing and the Medicare Act another. When it comes to specifying the details of coverage, human or natural rights won't take us very far. The right to access to your credit report raises a similar problem. How could this be a human or natural right? We would first need to say that there was something intrinsically human or natural about the practice of extending credit—which is extremely doubtful. Though it is a common practice, societies have done without it, and apparently without dehumanizing their numbers. In fact, it is computer technology which occasions the agitation for this right. And if the right is expressed in terms of access to computer banks, it rings a little hollow to say that one demands the right in the name of the human species. In support of specific demands, the language of human and natural rights runs the risk of sounding merely rhetorical. To apply the strategy where it is not appropriate may possibly end up discrediting it. And agreement about which rights are the human or natural ones is so hard to come by that this is no small risk.

The second strategy for using rights in a campaign to promote social change involves arguing that rights which others in the society enjoy should be extended to one's own group as well. The most familiar use of this strategy in this country is found in the constitutional arguments which invoke the "equal protection" clause of the Fourteenth Amendment. Those who use this sort of argument begin by appealing to values which are accepted and acknowledged by the society at large but which are not promoted for everyone alike. Rights are demanded to secure these values for a group which currently does not enjoy them. That requires showing that there is no good reason to treat the discriminated-against-group differently. For where there are good reasons, discrimination is neither invidious nor socially unacceptable. In fact, we don't really call the recognition of legitimate differences discrimination at all. So the strategy aims to show that those demanding their rights are similar to those who already have them in the relevant respects.

The U.S. Supreme Court argued in this way when it ordered the desegregation of public schools in *Brown v. Board of Education*. They reasoned that segregation led to feelings of inferiority in black children which interfered with their capacity to participate fully in civic life (military, politics, etc.). Since there is no relevant difference between blacks and whites *as citizens*, and since a segregated education creates differences in this respect, blacks have an equal right to what whites already have (an education which does not instill feelings of inferiority). The Court did not say that every human had a right to education. It said that if the States supplied a service that was essential for participation in society to some groups, they had to supply it to all groups which were entitled to participate.

A similar strategy was adopted by many who supported the reduction of the voting age from 21 to 18 years. They certainly did not want to be put in the position of holding that all humans have the right to vote. Nor were they willing to try to convince a preponderance of the American people that this would be a better society if the youth could vote, too. The arguments usually focused on the similarities between 18 year olds as a group and the over-21-year-olds. The differences were made to seem minor and arbitrary in comparison to the fundamental similarities. By age 18 people are beginning to carve out their own lives, make their own decisions, work, pay taxes, and so on. They should not be denied the rights of others who do the same. The emphasis here is on the justice of the extension of the right.

The strength of this strategy lies in the fact that people within the society already accept the values which are to be protected by right. The society does not have to be convinced that education or the vote is a good thing. The movement for social change does not challenge the basic outlook of the society in this way. The difficulty, rather, is to get people to see similarities where they have previously seen differences. It is no easy task to convince a racist that blacks are like him, or a male chauvinist that women have similar needs and desires, for this kind of argument tends to challenge people's basic perceptions on rational grounds. It shows them that they cannot express in words differences which they feel—and goes on to discount those feelings as prejudice or warped sensibilities. So in spite of a communality of values at the general level, the opponents of the extension of rights must eventually be discredited in the name of justice.

The third major strategy in a campaign to establish rights involves arguing that the society would be better off if it decided to treat the group in question in a new way. The rights are specified and acknowledged in order to institutionalize the new form of relationship. Here the appeal is not to values currently ensconced, but to people's sense of progress and social improvement. Rights advocates hold out the vision of society as it could be, rather than society as it is for some, to try to win their demands. This strategy seems to rely more than the others on the good will of the discriminating group. In that sense it does not provide much leverage in head to head confrontations. Most discrimination is not inadvertent, and most discriminators do not see eye to eye with those advocating social change about what would count as progress. It is hard to imagine, for example, trying to convince an employer that employees have a right to a thirty-hour work week, on the grounds that it would promote a more leisurely and relaxed society. Self-interest aside, it is doubtful that the employer would regard this as a vision of a better society. She or he would more likely call it decadent and degenerate.

Where this strategy is of use is in enlisting the support of third parties who might be able to help bring about the change. People who were concerned with child welfare in the nineteenth century supported compulsory education legislation designed to limit child labor. They were not saying that children had a natural right to education, or that children should be given what others had. They claimed that it would be better for the children and for society at large if the children had some respite from the grind of life in the factory. The industrialists did not share this view, but there was sufficient support in other quarters that legislation was passed. The right to compulsory education initiated new standards for child labor.

Each of these strategies has its uses and its moments. Some movements for social change invoke them all. It is important for us to be aware that these can be tactical decisions. That does not mean that they are bad tactics; it just means that we will have to examine the claims which are made in behalf of each proposed right rather carefully to make sure the right is well and properly grounded. But having looked at the ways in which groups can go about arguing for their rights, we need now to look a little more closely at what sorts of things they are arguing for. What rights should children have? In the following chapters we shall consider some of the rights which are being demanded on behalf of children. We can look at them in the context of the grounds on which they are being advocated: human or natural rights, social justice, or social benefit. This will be useful because we are interested in more than just a list of rights or an assessment of their impact on our contemporary social life. We also need to know the extent to which the need for social change is pressing.

CHAPTER III

Human Rights

The clearest and most straightforward statement of children's rights as human rights is to be found in the United Nations Declaration of the Rights of the Child. After reaffirming its faith in "fundamental human rights and in the dignity and worth of the human person," the document goes on to list what children are entitled to in ten principles. These are summarized as follows:

1. the enjoyment of the rights mentioned, without any exception whatsoever, regardless of race, color, sex, religion, or nationality;
2. special protection, opportunities, and facilities to enable them to develop in a healthy and normal manner, in freedom and dignity;
3. a name and a nationality;
4. social security, including adequate nutrition, housing, recreation, and medical services;
5. special treatment, education, and care if handicapped;
6. love and understanding and an atmosphere of affection and security, in the care and under the responsibility of their parents whenever possible;
7. free education and equal opportunity to develop their individual abilities;
8. prompt protection and relief in times of disaster;
9. protection against all forms of neglect, cruelty, and exploitation;
10. protection from any form of racial, religious, or other discrimination, and an upbringing in a spirit of peace and universal brotherhood.[1]

It is worth noticing that these rights have mostly to do with the protection of the child, and as such they are very different from the list proposed by Richard Farson (cited in Chapter I) and other contemporary children's rights advocates. For, unlike Farson, the drafters of this declaration focus on the "physical and mental immaturity" of children and their attendant need for "special safeguards and care." This assumption will be important for us later when we come to examine the adequacy of this list, but for now we need to look at the idea that these rights belong to children as human rights.

There is no question that the appeal to human rights makes this Declaration very attractive as a political manifesto. In the first place, to call them human rights is to say that all humans have them regardless of where they live or when they lived. In short, these rights belong to people everywhere and for all time. If this is so, then the Declaration is not saying that children should be given these rights; it is saying that children *already have them*. Insofar as there are children in the world who don't actually receive the treatment specified in the Declaration, they can be seen as having their rights withheld from them. This way of seeing things makes the Declaration more urgent. If children are systematically and continuously having their rights violated, it is a cause for great concern. It is much more compelling than a situation in which a group of people are trying to convince others that they should create these rights for children. In those circumstances, there is more justification for slow deliberation and foot-dragging.

Another advantage to the human rights approach to these demands is that it does not get bogged down in arguments about different value systems in different cultures. Many items on the United Nations' list are not recognized as entitlements everywhere in the world; for example, free education and recreation. But the fact that some cultures do not think of these things as rights does not necessarily mean they are not rights—even in those cultures. By claiming that these rights belong to people *as human beings*, the Declaration is claiming that some cultures may be denying to their members rights which are more basic and more fundamental than even the values of the culture. In the face of this, the argument that the rights do not belong to children because they are not recognized in the culture would be inadequate. The admission becomes a criticism of the culture itself, rather than a reason to ignore the Declaration.

A third strength of the human rights strategy is that it rallies maximum support for the Declaration. Because the rights are said to belong to all human beings, every human being has a stake in their enforcement. A violation of your human rights is a threat to me in a way that a violation of some of your other rights may not be. Suppose that people in another part of the world have a statutory right to use alcoholic beverages, and that this right is revoked through a legitimate governmental action. That situation really would not affect me at all. No principle is involved which transcends their local boundaries. If, on the other hand, one of their human rights were violated (human rights are usually thought of as the kind of thing that cannot be revoked), I should be concerned. For it is a right which I have, too, and the principle that one of *my* rights may not be taken away or ignored has been challenged. In this way, human rights issues are global rather than local, and defenders of human rights can seek support anywhere in the world.

The foundation of these strengths of the human rights strategy for social change is the assumption that there are universally acknowledged moral values. These values are universal because they are derived from the basic characteristics of human beings, and they are acknowledged—at least implicitly—because we all can recognize what it is that makes for a fellow member of the human species. If this assumption is correct, then wherever and whenever there are human beings there are certain things which they are entitled to—no matter what the specific circumstances of their lives might be. Whether the United Nations has put its collective finger on the things that human children are entitled to is the question we must now consider. In the course of answering this question, we will have to answer another: Is it helpful to think of children's rights as human rights at all?

How Can You Find Your Human Rights?

The search for human rights usually begins with the search for the "essence" of humanity. We needn't worry too much about what the word "essence" means. As a practical matter, the search is directed toward those things which human beings share with one another and which, at the same time, set them apart from other animals and things. This test rules out characteristics which only some human beings have—like white skin. It also rules out characteristics which some animals have—like the ability to feel and express pain. There will also be characteristics which are not ruled out by this test but which, nevertheless, will not take us very far toward establishing human rights. We cannot make much of the fact that we have a very unique sort of kidney, for example. The application of this test with an eye toward human rights has standardly yielded three candidates for the essential human feature: Reason, Freedom, and Human Dignity.

Reason is the capacity to think. That is, to calculate, to abstract, to use logic, and so on. One usually refers to the higher levels of intelligence here so as to exclude clever animals. We might worry about setting the standards too high and excluding some people, but for our purposes, that order of intelligence which requires the use of a language will probably do the trick. Freedom is the capacity to make choices. It should not be thought of as simply an alternative candidate to reason for the human essence, for making choices requires planning and deliberation, and these are types of reasoning. But freedom goes beyond reason insofar as it also requires taking action. A being that makes choices cannot merely passively react to situations; it must initiate one choice from a range of options. Human dignity, too, builds on the capacities to think and sometimes make choices. It is the capacity to recognize the moral value of one's self and other persons. This is usually expressed in terms of treating people as "ends in themselves." Defenders of human rights have picked out any or all of these characteristics as the essential features of humanity. There is no need to rely on one of them exclusively. But we do need to go on to ask: What is the significance of these features?

If these characteristics of human beings were merely interesting facts about us, there would be little more to say. After all, everything is different from everything else, so each thing and each kind of thing is bound to have some unique features which set it apart. But the proponents of human rights do not treat these characteristics as mere facts. They are also said to be the source of our fundamental values. Insofar as we value our humanity, we should value reason, freedom, and/or human dignity. What is being said here is that we are not (would not be) human beings without one or more of the features. And being a human being is not only something we are—it is something we want to be. The wanting it gives it its value. Since all of us are presumed to value our humanity, and since we could not have it without reason, freedom and/or human dignity, these things are more than mere facts about us. They are significant as our species identity.

Having established the importance of the essentially human features, the next step in finding your human rights is to ask: What does a person require in order to acquire and maintain reason, freedom, and human dignity? For what is required will also be what a person is entitled to—given the importance of being human to humans.

The answers which have been given to this question since the seventeenth century—when it started to be asked with regularity —have been quite similar. John Locke (in 1691) identified our human rights (he called them natural rights, but more on that later) as life, liberty and property. In the Declaration of Independence of the United States (1776), they are life, liberty and the pursuit of happiness. In the Declaration of the Rights of Man and of Citizens from the French Revolution (1789), they are liberty, property, security, and resistance to oppression. Contemporary thinking on this matter runs along similar lines. The United Nations Declaration of Human Rights (1948) cites life, liberty, and security of person. In 1955, H. L. A. Hart, a legal philosopher, suggests the equal right of all men to be free. In 1973 Joel Feinberg, another philosopher, mentions the right to goods that cannot be in scarce supply, such as equal protection of the law, the right not to be treated inhumanely, and the right not to be subjected to exploitation or degradation.[2] It is fairly easy to see the technique that is at work here. Try to imagine the circumstances that would undermine the acquisition or maintenance of reason, freedom, and/or human dignity. People will require—and be entitled to—those things which would allow them to avoid these circumstances. For example, you cannot reason if you are dead, so you have a right to life. You cannot make choices if others can always tell you what to do, so you have a right to liberty. The reader will, no doubt, be able to carry out the rest of the calculations and discover her or his human rights.

The fundamental rights which we are discussing here are sometimes called natural rights rather than human rights. In most cases there is not much difference between the rights which are human and those which are natural, but the stories about how it is that one has them differ considerably. These variations are important when it comes to considering the value of this strategy for demanding children's rights, so I shall describe the natural rights story briefly.

Where the human rights story begins with the contemplation of the typical human being as an isolated person, the natural rights story begins with the individual in a society—any society will do. Many of the rights which a person has are created by the society and bear its stamp. In our society, the right to vote in national elections at age 18, the right to bear arms, and the right to apply for a driver's license are examples of such rights. Many other rights as well are the product of local custom, law, and governmental rules and regulations. Now all of these rights can be abstracted away—by an act of imagination—if we try to think of what life would be like without any rule-making body (informal as well as formal). To do this is to work ourselves back to the "State of Nature"—a state of anarchy, but not necessarily of disorder. There is no recognized authority which can make rules and enforce them. The state of nature, it is argued, is *not* a state without rights. After one peels away those rights which are the product of social custom and law, there still remains a body of rights to which each individual is still entitled. For even in a state of nature, people would maintain some basic social relationships, and the maintenance of those relationships would require some rules for the treatment of others. We are entitled to have others follow those rules. Since we have a right to this even in a state of nature, the rules are called natural law, and our attendant rights are natural rights.

Both the human rights and the natural rights stories have

their critics. A main source of criticism, and continuing point of debate, has to do with the possibility of deriving values from facts about human beings. As we saw, that was a crucial step in the human rights story, and it has been attacked as sleight of hand. The fact that things are a certain way does not mean they *ought* to be, the critics have said. The jump from "is" to "ought" is made with values which people draw from their own social experience. The question is not "What are humans in isolation entitled to?," for humans in isolation literally have no values. All values, and therefore, all rights, are ultimately social phenomena. As Jeremy Bentham put it in his scathing criticism of "The Declaration of the Rights of Man and of Citizens:"

. . . no habit of obedience, and thence no government—no government, and thence no laws—no laws, and thence no such things as rights—no security—no property . . .[3]

Bentham goes on to say that rights can never take precedence over social needs (as they would if they were human or natural rights). If society and government are the source of all rights, then "there is no right which, when the abolition of it is advantageous to society, should not be abolished."[4]

Although the concepts of human and natural rights are not universally accepted and problem-free, our purpose here is not to add to the criticism. We will stick to the question of whether these concepts are very helpful for the children's rights movement. In particular, are they grounds for the rights which are listed in the United Nations Declaration of the Rights of the Child?

There is an initial problem with treating many of these rights as human rights, and that is the problem of vagueness. "Social security," "special treatment," "education," "recreation," and "relief" are all fairly vague terms. They do not spell out in any precise way just what children are entitled to. Some further detail is supplied in the full statement of principles, but even here much is left unsaid. For example, the right to education is developed as "free and compulsory, at least in the elementary stages." In Principle 7, it further states that the child "shall be given an education which will promote his general culture, and enable him on a basis of equal opportunity to develop his abilities, his individual judgment, and his sense of moral and social responsibility, and to become a useful member of society." As a model of precision, this statement leaves a great deal to be desired, but ironically, as a statement of the child's *human* rights, it may have said too much, for human rights need to be vague.

Vagueness is an endemic problem for human or natural rights because of the need to begin from the lowest common denominator of human values. Unless one begins with characteristics or basic relationships which all or virtually all human beings share, the derived right may be challenged as applying to only some humans (i.e. those who happen to have the characteristics or relationships under discussion). The loss of universality would considerably weaken the impact of the human rights strategy as we have described it. The search for agreement in a world of diversity must of necessity avoid detail.

The importance of being vague is nicely illustrated in a story about the fundamental law (a related concept) which Christopher Hill reports in *The Century of Revolution*:

The beauty of the concept of fundamental law lay precisely in its vagueness and in the assumption that it was self-evident. All could agree about the importance of something that was never defined. In 1641 Strafford was impeached, among other charges, for subverting the fundamental laws of the kingdom. The Commons were just about to vote the charge when the witty and malicious Edmund Waller rose and, with seeming innocence, asked what the fundamental laws of the kingdom were. There was an uneasy silence. No-one dared to attempt a definition which would certainly have divided the heterogeneous majority, agreed only in its view that for Strafford, stone dead hath no fellow. The situation was saved by a lawyer who leapt to his feet to say that if Mr. Waller did not know what the fundamental laws of the kingdom were, he had no business to be sitting in the house.[5]

We can see how vagueness becomes a problem for the United Nations Declaration if we consider the right to "adequate nutrition . . . and medical services" in Principle 4. What is adequate nutrition? Is it enough food to keep a person alive and functioning? Or perhaps enough food to keep children from becoming ill because of their diet? Or is it sufficient food to enable a child to lead an active and vigorous life? Again, we might try to specify a diet in terms of its vitamin, mineral, protein, carbo-hydrate, and fat content. This would be difficult because research is still going on in the area of nutrition, and claims made now about what the child has a right to might well have to be revised later. But even if that were not a problem, does the child have a right to a minimal diet, or to something more? And, of course, we should not lose sight of the fact that the standards of what constitutes a good diet vary in different cultures.

All of these same problems can be raised in terms of medical services, too. Do children have a right to inoculation against contagious diseases? A right to emergency treatment? To reg-ular medical care? A right to advanced life-saving technology (such as access to dialysis machines)? The more detail one includes here, the more likely it is that the right will have to be stated in terms consistent with the level of knowledge and wealth of a particular society at a particular time. Children in twen-tieth century America may have a right to polio vaccine, but it makes no sense to say this of children in thirteenth century England. And that makes it highly dubious that the right to polio vaccine is a human right—even if we still want to say that the right to medical services is. To treat these rights as human rights means that we shall have to defer to the lowest common denominator effect. That is, we shall have to leave them vague enough to avoid making them dependent on what any particular society is able to provide.

The trouble with all this is that the vagueness of the human rights considerably weakens their impact on the lives of children. In Chapter 2, I emphasized that if rights are to be meaningful they must be precise enough to spell out what others must or must not do. The aim of a rights campaign is to restructure existing social relationships so that children will be treated in new and more satisfactory ways. To do this, it is important to limit the discretion with which others may interpret these new relationships. The more discretion they have, the more likely they will be to continue in the old ways, or give the rights a minimal interpretation. What else should we expect from those who did not see the point of restructuring our relations to children in the first place? Because human rights lack this precision, they do not tend to be very demanding.

Beyond vagueness, there is a second substantial difficulty with treating children's rights as human rights. The problem is that children are not unequivocally regarded as human. Odd as this sounds, most defenders of human rights have not intended them to apply to children. As Herbert Morris puts it:

Children possess the right to be treated as persons but they possess this right as an individual might be said in the law of property to possess a future interest.[6]

In other words, they don't possess this right when they are children. The reason that children are treated as less than human when it comes to human rights is that they do not obviously have the characteristics which are said to belong to all humanity. Some children, anyhow, do not have the capacity to think, to make choices, or to recognize the moral dignity of themselves and of others. Babies clearly do not have these capacities, and it is at least arguable that the moral sense required for the third characteristic is not developed until adolescence.

For defenders of human rights, the choice has been between excluding children (along with the severely retarded and the senile) from the category of humanity on the one hand, and giving up reason, freedom, and/or human dignity as the essential features of humanity in favor of some less stringent test on the other. Under these circumstances, children are the inevitable losers. The criteria for humanity must have sufficient significance for humans to make them worth valuing. If they are too mundane, it will be difficult to generate any rights from them. And given the lowest common denominator problem, defenders of human rights do not want to water them down any more than they have to.

Nevertheless, it would be wrong to leave the impression that children without the human rights are simply to be treated as non-humans when they are children. Morris said that they do have a future interest in their human rights. Children are rather thought of as *potential* humans. They do not yet have the human capacities, but they are in the process of developing them. The difference here is subtle, and a bit more needs to be said about it.

The characteristics which give humans their value are not described as the *activities* of thinking, choosing and valuing others for their own sakes, because not all adults do these things. And certainly no adult does them all the time. But adults are able to do them in the sense that they have all the mental equipment for the job. If they do not use the equipment, so much the worse for them. Still, they have the *capacity* to do so. Now children are said to differ from adults in this regard to the extent that they do not yet have the mental equipment to reason, make choices, or recognize the moral dimension of humanity. They will develop these capacities if all goes well, but as children they only have them *potentially*. If a child and an adult are unreasonable, they are unreasonable in different ways. The child lacks the features which the adult fails to employ. At least, that is what the proponents of human or natural rights who would deny them to children would say.

Even if this is all true, it is still not necessary to give up on the idea of human rights for children entirely. Those human rights which they will have as adults may be put off into the indefinite future, but there are others which they still might have as children. If we can say that children are entitled to the chance to develop their human capacities, then they have as rights all of those things which are required for the development of those capacities. Alternatively, they have a right to be protected from those things which are likely to hinder the development of the human capacities. This is the line which is taken, for the most part, in the United Nations Declaration.

According to that document, children need rights because they are physically and mentally immature. Principles 2, 8, 9 and 10 refer explicitly to protection against various threats to life, health and security. The other principles demand for children rights to things which would be needed in the course of normal development: love and understanding, a sense of identity (name and nationality), the absence of discrimination. Included here are adequate nutrition, housing, recreation, and medical services, the lack of which would presumably hamper normal development. In short, these are rights that children have not because they are human, but because they can become human. The United Nations Declaration of the Rights of the

Child is a document squarely in the tradition of the caretaker ideology. Despite a reference to the contrary in Principle 2, it does not recognize children as being presently endowed with "freedom and dignity." In this way, too, the human rights strategy is of limited use to the children's movement. At best, it can be used to establish a baseline for the quality of our relations to children. And the children's rights movement is by now well past that point.

Another way to bring out this point is to ask whether children have a right to the *minimum* or the *optimum* of whatever is required for the development of their capacities. A right to the minimum is a right to the bare necessities which are required for development. The concern here is to ensure the fact of the development of each child's capacities, but it is not directed toward questions of quality —whether the development is adequate, good, or excellent. This does not mean that people who endorse minimal rights are uninterested in the quality of the child's development, but only that they do not think that quality is a matter of *right*. On this view, everyone has a right to a minimum, and some children are fortunate enough to receive more. By contrast, a right to the optimum is a right to as much as is required to ensure the fullest development for each child under the circumstances. To say that the child has a right to the optimum is to say that this course of development is not only desirable, it is obligatory. Here the issue is quality—the highest quality available within the limitations of the resources of the society in which the child lives.

A right to the minimum tends to be expressed in terms of obligations of non-interference. Others are obligated not to do anything which would interfere with the development of the child. On this version of children's rights excessive servitude, exploitation, and the withholding of life's essentials would be prohibited. Still, even scrupulous non-interference would leave most children well below the minimum necessary for their development (however we decided what that minimum was). Even here, some obligations of performance would have to be imposed. These are typically obligations binding the parents or the state to provide the tools of development: nutrition, shelter, educational materials, and so on. Also, insofar as children do not develop "naturally" if left to their own devices, a certain amount of guidance may be required from some adults, usually parents or appointed guardians. The important point to keep in mind here is that the interpretation of these rights as rights to a minimum tends to impose as few obligations of performance as possible. Under the interpretation of children's rights as rights to the optimum chance to develop the human capacities, many more obligations of performance tend to be imposed. It is possible to go overboard here and obligate adults to do too much. This could well have a smothering effect on the child and interfere with development. But this has not, historically, been a problem for the children's rights movement. Errors have been of omission rather than of excess. So while it is important for the optimum interpretation not to let the list of obligations on others get out of hand, the danger is not so severe that it should instinctively push us back to the minimum. The major problem for the optimum interpretation remains the search for what is actually required for optimal development of the human capacities. At present, nobody can say with much confidence.

A human rights strategy for children's rights best supports a minimum interpretation of those rights. The essential characteristics of humanity are the typical characteristics—those by which the members of the species are recognized as such. They are not the best within us or the most that members of our species are capable of. To define the species in terms of an ideal is to put the universality of the characterization in doubt, for our values are supposed to be derived from our essential features, and to state the ideal first is to begin with values and thereby turn the process around. The values which support such an ideal would no longer plausibly be said to have universal significance. The upshot of this is that we can only be said to have a human right to be typical, not superior. And from this we cannot generate anything more than a right to develop successfully—a minimal rather than an optimal development.

Another consideration which lends support to the minimal interpretation of the child's human rights is the fact that we are only now beginning to understand what is involved in optimal development. Our understanding itself, as well as the means of implementing it, depend crucially on the resources our society has available for use on this question. Not all societies do have or have had these resources; and it seems idle to insist that children have a right to things which are not known of in their society, and which could not be provided if they were. This does not mean that children do not have a right to optimal development in societies that understand and can afford it. But it means that this right is not likely to be called a human right. For again, human rights seek the lowest common denominator in order to arrive at a universality that transcends social differences. Every society has some version of medical services, and children are said to have a human right to them, but very few societies have the technology or the resources to provide dialysis machines to every child with kidney failure. Such machines may be required for the optimal development of some children. But if children in this society are entitled to access to those machines as a *human* right, then all children in all societies are. That would make a mockery of children's rights in the poorer and less technological societies. A human rights strategy cannot press for the optimum and retain the credibility of its claims to universality.

The question of whether there really are human or natural rights is not terribly important for the children's rights movement. On the assumption that there are such rights, they turn out to be vague, only indirectly applicable to children, and rather minimal in content. They do not take children's rights issues very much beyond questions of protection of the child. In this respect they will not even support all that the adherents to the caretaker conception of children's rights would demand. When we turn to the children's rights advocates who want to see us treat children as we treat adults, to acknowledge them a higher social status, to accord them greater freedom and dignity, it is hard to imagine how the appeal to human rights could be very helpful. So we should not be surprised to see that children's rights issues are treated primarily as issues of social justice or as a basis for social progress in the more recent materials on this subject. We should now turn our attention to those issues.

CHAPTER IV

Equal Rights as Social Justice

What rights should children have? This is a natural question to ask at this point, but it is the wrong one. To provide a list of children's rights is still to suggest that those rights are somehow different from the rights of adults. Putting the question this way does not yet really challenge the idea of a double standard of rights for children and adults. And that is precisely what I want to challenge now. As I see it, the campaign for children's rights should not try to establish a new set of rights for children, it should aim at the elimination of the distinction between adults and children when it comes to having rights.

Most of the rights which adults have in our society are established in law and enforceable in the courts. Many of these legal rights are also moral rights in the sense that they are codifications of our society's deeply-held, fundamental moral convictions. The rights not to be murdered or assaulted are of this sort, as is the right not to be a slave. Other rights have somewhat less to do with our fundamental moral principles and are more directly derived from our conceptions of government and political process. Our Constitutional rights which set limits on governmental power such as the rights to free press, free speech, freedom of religion, trial by jury, and due process of law, fall into this category. So do the rights to vote, stand for elective office, and remove elected officials. Finally there are rights which seek to establish custom in law or to create new customary practices through the law. Rights relating to marriage and divorce are of this type. Whatever their source, these rights are incorporated into our legal system and help structure the ways in which we must relate to one another. Taken as a whole, these constitute the bulk of the rights which adults have in any given society.[1] These rights may differ somewhat from place to place, but in any given place they set the standard for the way adults are treated. This is the standard which we must use to articulate the rights of children.

When we make something a right, we are indicating that we value it, and that it needs a special status because there are sometimes obstacles to enjoying it. A list of our rights is a list of our society's most cherished public values: free speech, a free press, strict procedures and due process in criminal court, no confiscation of property without compensation, the right to travel, the right to privacy, and so on. If we want these things so much for ourselves, why should we deny them to our children?

The last question is largely rhetorical, for it raises the problem but it does not settle it. The problem is the problem of the double standard which we have for our treatment of adults and children. The double standard is embedded deeply in our social practices, and it is well-established in our laws as well. There is one set of rights for adults and another for children. Adults' rights mostly provide them with opportunities to exercise their powers; children's rights mostly provide them with protection and keep them under adult control.

Now a double standard is not *necessarily* a bad thing. We would not, for example, want a single standard for judging gourmet chefs and institutional cooks. French cooking would not go over well at a boarding school in Montana, and macaroni and cheese would not win compliments at an intimate bistro in Manhattan. When we set standards, we need a sense of what is appropriate, and things which are apparently similar —like cooking—may not actually be so. In order to mark important differences, we need different standards.

But the more common story about double standards is that they are used to establish and maintain a privileged status for one group over another. This was true of the double standard of "literacy" used as a voting qualification in parts of this country prior to the 1964 Civil Rights Act. For whites, literacy meant being able to write your name; for blacks, it meant having to answer detailed questions about a state constitution. The practical outcome of this was obvious to all concerned. In light of the fact that double standards can be used to discriminate against groups of people—and often are used this way—our healthy scepticism and sense of reality ought to make us a little suspicious of the fact that the rights of children and adults are measured on different standards. If there is not a very good reason for the difference in treatment, then the double standard is unjust.

I am using the term "unjust" deliberately here because justice is precisely what is at stake. Justice has been called a "two-dimensional" concept.[2] It deals, on the one hand, with what people deserve. This is reflected in the phrase "just deserts." Our sense of justice is offended when people work hard and are not rewarded, and also when they do very little but nevertheless receive recognition, praise, or a lot of cash. The other side of the concept of justice deals with the question of equality and fair play. People should not be treated arbitrarily or capriciously. This dimension is expressed in our concept of equal protection of the laws. It is this dimension of justice which is at stake in the double standard problem.

Questions of social justice usually have to do with how the various benefits and burdens of living with others are distributed in a group. Is the distribution equal? Is it fair? Who gets what advantages? Who pays what costs? Does anyone who gives more get less, or *vice versa*? The basic principle of justice which governs these matters is ". . . like cases are to be treated alike and different cases are to be treated differently."[3] We can take this a little further by adding: "Treat people equally unless and until there is a justification for treating them unequally."[4] Neither of these principles is complete because neither says which likenesses and which differences are the relevant ones in each case. That is for us to figure out. Still, they are very useful principles since they tell us that *if* we cannot cite a relevant difference between two cases, we must treat them alike, and *if* we can, then we should treat them differently. For example, if everyone is allowed to park in front of city hall when they have business to do there, then it would be unjust to tow my car as long as I had business to do there too. But if I parked there to go shopping down the street, my case is relevantly different from everyone else's, and it is just to tow me away. Here it is easy to decide which similarities and which differences are relevant.

But what of the double standard of rights for adults and children? Is it unjust? If there are differences between adults and children which are relevant to granting rights to one group but not the other, then it is not unjust. But if the differences are not relevant, then the two groups are, and should be, treated alike. In other words, children are people, too. If they are people without relevant differences from other people, then they should have the same rights as others. Anything less would be an injustice.

When we call for equal rights for children—for an end to the double standard—we want the elimination of "child" as a separate category *in all aspects of life where the distinction is not relevant*. Of course, it is all right to treat people differently when there are good reasons to do so. I am not saying that nobody should have a right unless everyone has it. That would amount to applying blinders to the possibility of relevant differences among people. What I am saying is that unless relevant differences can be demonstrated, it is not right to treat people differently; it is unjust. In my view the differences between adults and children, such as they are, have been way overstated by those who support the double standard. Children are presumed to be weak, passive, mindless, and unthinking; adults are presumed to be rational, highly motivated, and efficient. The picture is drawn too sharply, of course, and nobody pretends that there are not exceptions. The trouble, however, is that a decent account of equal rights for children cannot be based on the exceptions. If it is, we have only readjusted the double standard; we have not eliminated it.

This point is important because much of the recent agitation for children's rights has depended quite heavily on the demonstrated capabilities of *some* children (to vote, to be emancipated from their parents, and so on). We might appreciate the progress that can be made in this way, but we also need to be aware of the limitations of this strategy. In this chapter I want to expose the arbitrariness of the distinction between children and adults. It should be clear, however, that I am doing this to show that the objection to this arbitrariness is not very devastating—unless we are also willing to say that the acknowledged differences are irrelevant to the question of extending rights to children.

"People are people" we say, meaning that we are all alike in that respect at least. Another platitude of equal significance is that everyone is a unique individual. We can go in either direction here, and that shows that there are no overwhelming and compelling similarities or differences which will allow us to decide whether we need to treat children and adults in the same way or not. What we need to do is to look at the differences which people typically cite when they reject certain rights for children. How relevant are they? Children are all younger than adults, to be sure, but that by itself is hardly relevant. Rather, the argument goes, youth means a certain lack of maturity, and so a lack of a variety of *capacities*. The list of capacities which children are supposed not to have varies depending on who is reciting it, but fundamentally it includes the capacities which we earlier called "essentially human." That is, the capacity to think or reason, to make choices, and to recognize the moral dignity of others. These may be expressed differently: the capacity to look out for oneself, to be persuaded by argument, to follow one's own self-interest, to accept social responsibilities, to be self-supporting, to accept the consequences of one's actions, and so on.

When we say that someone has these things as capacities, we are making a judgment about whether they could do certain things which they do not happen to be doing at the time. These judgments are a little obscure, but we can clarify the point of making them with a fairly non-controversial example about a physical capacity. The average one-year-old child has the potential to swim 25 yards, but not the capacity. We say this because she does not have the skills, the coordination, or the stamina to do so. With practice and conditioning the child could do so —many will. We are assuming, of course, that there is nothing about her *now* which will make this task impossible in the future. If she had certain kinds of physical defects, discernible hydrophobia, and so on, we would say that she did not even have the potential to swim the 25 yards. In the absence of these things, we judge her to have the potential, but not the capacity, and this is so even if she never learns to swim.

Some five-year-old children have the capacity to swim 25 yards. They have the skills, the coordination, and the stamina. Now we may judge that some particular child has this capacity even though the child has not recently swum this distance, and even if the child does not do so upon request. For when we say someone has a capacity, we are saying something about what she *could* do. If the child does not swim that distance, we would need to know the reason. Suppose she stopped swimming from choice, from boredom, from having too many other things to do, or from a lack of opportunity. We would judge that she still had the capacity. If she became severely disabled, or if swimming were the sort of thing you could not do unless you kept it up, we would probably say that she lost the capacity. The point is that a person does not have to do a particular thing constantly in order to have the capacity to do it—the capacity is there or not, depending upon why that person is not doing it.

This point is important because many adults do not actually do what they are said to be capable of doing—like voting, or joining associations, or looking out for their own interests, or being persuaded by arguments. But they are presumed to fail at these things, when they do, for reasons different from those that explain why children fail. Adults fail because of circumstances or choice; children are said to fail of necessity. That is, they are supposed to lack an essential element of success: a capacity.

The story that children and adults differ in this way is widely accepted and commonly believed. These capacities are assumed to match pretty closely with age. Younger people do not have them, and older people do. In fact, it is quite difficult to make this point very accurately. It is relatively easy and quite a bit of fun to show that this position is rather arbitrary and more than a little prejudiced.

Anyone who wishes to say that some people but not others should have a particular right must, of necessity, draw a line. Everyone on one side of the line has the right; everyone on the other side does not. There cannot be a group of people for whom the question of whether or not they have the right is left unsettled. For to leave it unsettled is in effect to deny them the right. So wherever the line is drawn, it must be drawn precisely.

The rights we are discussing are rights for which the line is drawn according to age. A person has the right to vote on her or his eighteenth birthday. Nobody has it before they are eighteen, and everyone but an alien or convicted felon does thereafter. Different rights are assigned at different ages in different states. Some people may marry without parental permission at age sixteen; others at age eighteen, or older. Prior to the Twenty-seventh Amendment to the Constitution, the right to vote was given to eighteen-, nineteen-, twenty-, and twenty-one-year-olds in various states. The rights to own property and contract debts are also conferred at various specific ages to various people. The variability of the age of majority is a clue to the arbitrary nature of the line-drawing here, but it should not be given too much significance. Even if there were only one age of majority for all rights in all states, it too would be arbitrary. *Any* line which uses age to distinguish people with rights from people without can be shown to be arbitrary.

The reason for the arbitrariness is this: We always need a precise line to divide those with rights from those without. But it is impossible to draw a precise line between childhood and adulthood, for growing up is a developmental process, and there is never a moment at which someone who did not have one of the adult capacities suddenly acquires it. Not all changes are like this, of course, and so not all lines are arbitrary. Some changes in people are quite abrupt, like the change from life to death. Even here there are some cases which are hard to decide, but when the legal problems are set aside, the line between life and death is fairly precise and not very arbitrary. The same can be said for the line between winter and spring, if we go by the vernal equinox rather than the weather. The line marks a clear and recognizable change in the relationship between sun and earth.

Many changes are much less sudden and much less sharply defined. There is no point at which a piece of fruit is suddenly ripe or a tree is suddenly bare of leaves for the winter. There are moments when the tree is obviously bare just as surely as there are moments when it was quite fully covered with leaves. But there is a time every autumn when it is in transition, and it would be arbitrary to say "Now it is bare." In fact, we do not even try to draw a line here. For one thing, we have no need to do so. No purpose would be served if we did. And, for another, we realize that any point we picked would be arbitrary in the sense that we could have picked a point with a few more or a few less leaves with equal justice. There was nothing very special about any point we might settle on.

The change from childhood to adulthood is a process of gradual change like the ripening of fruit or the losing of leaves. Capacities are not acquired at a moment but developed over time. A newborn clearly does not reason; a normal sixteen-year-old clearly does. But what about the normal seven-year-old, or five-year-old, or three-year-old? Who would want to pick the age at which the child attains the capacity to reason? With children, unlike trees, we do not simply acknowledge a period of transition. Instead we draw lines, and we do so in part because we need to separate those with rights from those without. As we saw, designating rights requires drawing lines. So we say that the age of reason is eighteen. We do this and expose our line-drawing to the hazards of the slippery slope.

The slippery slope is an argument technique designed to move people off of their lines. It works like this: Suppose someone says that the age at which a person should have the right to vote is eighteen. The advocate of the eighteen-year-old vote may have good reasons to back up this position. Eighteen-year-olds are able to understand the issues, inform themselves, see the meaning of elections, have positions on national or local policies, accept equally important responsibilities in other areas of social life and so on. Whatever the reasons—in fact, for any reason—we can always ask: Is there really a significant difference here between someone who is eighteen years old, and someone who is seventeen years and 364 days old? Is the difference significant enough so that one should have the right that is denied to the other? I think that it is obvious that if we are comparing the typical eighteen-year-old with the typical seventeen-year-364-day-old person, that there will be no expressible relevant difference. There may be differences among two hand-picked individuals of these respective ages, but we are speaking of giving rights to groups on the basis of age here, so we must look at typical cases. And when we do, nothing that is said on behalf of the eighteen-year-old could not be said on behalf of the seventeen-year-364-day-old.

Once the advocate of the eighteen-year-old's right to vote admits that there is no significant difference among people two days apart in age, that person has made the first move down the slippery slope. The next step is obvious: Is there any relevant difference between the person who is seventeen years 364 days old and the person who is seventeen years 362 days old? Again development is a gradual process and significant changes do not turn up so quickly, especially in the typical case. If eighteen-year-olds should have the right to vote, so should seventeen-year-364-day-olds. And if they should have the right to vote, so should seventeen-year-362-day-olds, for there is no expressible difference among these groups, either.

I am sure that the reader has by now gathered that there is no expressible difference between a typical seventeen-year-362-day-old person and a typical seventeen-year-360-day-old person. Again, if the former should have the vote, so should the latter. The argument, as one can see, moves inexorably toward the newborn. The slope is gradual but nonetheless slippery for that. Notice that we are never in the position of claiming that the seventeen- or sixteen- or fifteen-year-old is just like the eighteen-year-old. The technique of the argument is first to establish the right for those just below the cut-off point, and then to argue that the next lowest group is like the one immediately above it. Still, the argument is only compelling to a point. Eventually it strains our credibility.

We all know quite well that the reasons for giving the right to vote to eighteen-year-olds do not apply with equal force to six-year-olds. And if that should be disputed, they surely do not apply to two-year-olds. So even though we cannot pick out differences between the typical fifteen-year-244-day-old and the typical fifteen-year-242-day-old, that does not mean that we cannot make more crude distinctions. Ultimately, the slippery slope only shows the arbitrariness of drawing any particular line; it does not show that there is no point in drawing rough distinctions. Your typical two-year-old cannot read, count change, cook dinner, and so on, while your typical sixteen-year-old can. These are differences in capacities—and they really are differences. An argument which tried to show that no children lacked the capacities of eighteen-year-olds would be crazy. But it is far from crazy to point out that those who insist on a sharp cut-off point when handing out rights base that insistence on an inaccurate assumption about the connection between age and capacities.

Once the opponents of equal rights for children have conceded the arbitrariness of the line they have drawn, the door is open for all kinds of exceptions on an individual basis. So far we have focused on the typical representative of any given age (the average sixteen-year 27-day-old). The actual fluctuation of the relationship between age and capacities on an individual case-by-case basis is much greater than the difference expressed as averages. Some fourteen-year-olds are incredibly able—by any standard. They have developed all their capacities as well as any typical adult. Some twenty-five-year-olds are not yet adult in any important sense of the word save the legal one. By hand-picking the examples, one can turn the age requirement against the opponents of children's rights. What objection could they have to granting rights to any individual who meets all of the relevant criteria and only fails to meet the arbitrary one of age? For age was only supposed to be an indicator of capacity in the first place. Shouldn't these people be willing to grant exceptions on a case-by-case basis?

When the argument reaches this stage, people who wish to withhold rights from children will often try to soften the impact of their arbitrariness. They concede that—ideally—exceptions should be made for children who are exceptionally mature with respect to the relevant capacities. If a child has demonstrated the ability to handle money wisely, then that child should have her or his own bank account, line of credit, and chance to buy on the budget plan. By admitting that children should be admitted into the realm of adult rights in the most blatant cases, the hard-liners soften sufficiently to make the injustice involved seem less serious. Of course, it is impossible and unrealistic to draw an absolutely precise line between those who should have a particular right and those who should not. But if the line is more or less accurate, and if exceptions are made for the most obvious cases, why should anyone complain?

Although this line of reasoning goes some way toward easing the injustice of strict line-drawing, it largely pays only lip service to the concept of equal rights for even some children. For while it would be nice to give the most able children their rights, as a practical matter, the legal mechanisms required to do this would probably not be workable. There are basically two ways we could try to do this. One is to grant as a *privilege* to the exceptionally underaged what adults have as a right; the other is to establish an agency with the power to confer rights on a case by case basis. The injustices done to children by denying them some rights would pale in comparison to those caused by problems involved in either proposal.

Suppose that we wanted to offer to some children—those with proper capacities—the privilege of doing or having what adults do or have by right. That is, we could extend to those children who were ready—at adult discretion—what adults claim simply because they are adults. The content of the child's privilege would be identical to the content of the adult's right. The child, however, would make her or his claim by a different route: through privilege rather than through right.

There are a couple of problems with this. The first is that privileges are *not* simply rights by a different route. They are much more precarious than that. Privileges are rather easily withdrawn if the behavior of those who have them is not pleasing to those who grant them. The problem is particularly acute here, since children have to demonstrate to adults that they have the necessary capacities. A choice on the part of the child which is in fundamental opposition to the wishes of the privilege-granting adult will be taken as evidence that the child does not really have the capacity to exercise the right. If another adult decides to take a vacation rather than fix a leaky roof, we are not likely to say that she or he is incapable of making a choice here—even if we think that that person made the wrong choice. With children, however, our first inclination is to say that it was no choice at all. Instead we say that the child is not yet able to choose—and cite the desire to take the vacation as evidence. As long as the exercise of the privilege is under the continuing scrutiny of adults, it will not function as a right should. We need our rights precisely because we are entitled to make choices which others may disapprove of, and we need a mechanism which prevents potential interlopers from becoming obstacles. "Privilege" is not up to the task.

There is also a logistical problem here. Who will do the granting? In some cases, the answer is fairly obvious. The privilege of using a family car or a portion of the family money is pretty strictly a family matter. Whoever grants privileges in the household would grant these. But what of those privileges which affect the rest of society? Suppose we are speaking of the privilege of being out of the home at any hour in an area which has a curfew for minors. Could a parent grant this privilege, or should it be the local police chief? What if the police chief granted it over the parent's objections? Other situations become even more complicated. If a child wishes to work, there are parents, an employer, perhaps a union and a school board and the state (as the regulator of labor practices) involved. Who may grant the privilege? Must they all agree? How are disagreements to be resolved? I do not think there is much point in trying to answer these questions very carefully. Disputes are bound to crop up early and often. In order to settle them, we would have to resort to a more formal mechanism for establishing who has a privilege and who does not. And once we have dispensed with informality, then we might as well think of conferring *rights* on a case by case basis. Would we want an agency —call it a Board of Competence—to do that?

Let us try to imagine what it would be like to confer rights on the basis of competence rather than age. In the first place, once it is conceded that possession of a capacity of some sort is the real criterion for granting certain rights, then those rights should be denied to *anyone* lacking the capacity. In other words, the criterion should be applied to adults with the same strictness with which it is applied to children. If moderately capable children are denied a right, moderately capable adults should be denied it as well. To do less would be to reintroduce the double standard in a new way—and all the injustice implied by that.

And we are now searching for ways to avoid the injustice of the double standard. Now, in fact, those who would deny equal rights to children do not advocate revoking the rights of less-than-competent adults. I think this reveals the depth of the double standard and the sort of arbitrariness that is at the bottom of it. But although it is revealing, it is probably not devastating. We can imagine that some of the people who think certain rights should be based on having the relevant capacities would be willing to make their positions consistent by advocating that adults be denied those rights where they do not have the appropriate competence.

The Board of Competence, then, would be in the business of certifying everyone for the capacity to exercise their rights. We can suppose that a person would be certified in the way we are now licensed to drive a car. There might be a written test, a personal interview, or some kind of practical demonstration. Perhaps we would have to be recommended by a couple of people who already had their rights. The exact details can be left to those with a taste for utopian fantasy. It is a safe bet that most of us are repelled by the possibility. The problems with this idea are immense. At a minimum we would expect uniform standards if we really wanted to insure against arbitrariness and injustice. Given our experience with government agencies, it is hard for most of us to be anything but sceptical about the benefits of such an agency. The cost in terms of inconvenience, red tape, and the like would be quite high; but it is the political dangers that are the real threat. The idea of letting the government hand out rights on an individual basis using criteria which would inevitably be vague and nebulous (what is the capacity to reason or make choices, anyhow?) calls up all kinds of opportunities for pay-offs and favoritism on the one hand, and for suppression of dissidents on the other. One need only remember the work of the draft boards during the height of the Viet Nam War to imagine what this would be like. If this is what it would take to do justice to children, the cost is probably too high.

A social injustice cannot be assessed in a vacuum. Our desire to eliminate it must always be measured against the cost of the possible alternative policies. In this case the social cost of resorting to a Board of Competence is probably higher than the cost of setting an arbitrary age limit for the granting of rights. That is, less injustice would no doubt be done when rights were granted by a mechanical process rather than as a result of official judgment. This is only a prediction, of course, but I for one would not want to set up the Board to see if it would work. The slippery slope argument shows that it is relatively unjust to use age as the criterion for conferring rights. Yet until we can come up with a way to confer them which is relatively *less* unjust, the objection is not very compelling. The fact that the development of an individual's capacities does not correlate very precisely with age will not take us very far toward equal rights for children. At best it will extend rights to some children; at worst it would lead to handing out some rights on a case-by-case basis.

Throughout this discussion we have been assuming that the possession of certain capacities was relevant to the possession of rights. That is, if people did not have those capacities, then they were sufficiently different from the people who did that they should be treated differently. That is the formal principle of justice. After we make allowances for the arbitrariness of the cut-off points, the assumption still does what it is intended to do. It separates adults and children into two categories and justifies allocating different rights to each. The slippery slope argument requires that we qualify this assumption of the relevance of the capacities in the implementation of rights, but it does not require us to abandon it.

In my view it is necessary to abandon the assumption that a person must have certain relevant capacities in order to have rights—even rights which seem to depend directly on the capacities in question—if we are going to make a strong commitment to equal rights for children. What makes the denial of equal rights for children unjust is not that there are no differences between children and adults, but rather that the differences are *not* relevant when it comes to conferring rights. This is the position I will now defend, and the best way to begin is to examine the assumption that a person must be presumed capable of exercising a right *on her or his own initiative* in order to have it. Why should that be so?

CHAPTER V

Borrowed Capacities

Let us assume that some rights, anyhow, require the use of certain capacities if they are to be exercised in a meaningful way. Does that mean that the person who has the right must also have the relevant capacities? At first glance, it may seem obvious that the person must have these capacities. But on reconsideration, it is far from obvious; in fact, I would say that it is simply false. What makes it seem so obvious is that we typically think of rights in terms of non-interference: If a person has a right to something, then everyone else has an obligation not to interfere with that person's having or doing that thing. A person is pretty much left alone with rights understood in this way. Lacking the capacities, the person lacks what is needed to exercise the right. But not all rights are understood in this way. Some rights are better expressed in terms of a principle of performance: If a person has a right to something, then someone has an obligation to help that person have or do that thing. When we think of rights in this way, we can see that a person without the relevant capacities may still have certain rights as long as someone who has the capacities can be obligated to help the person with the right. In other words, the principle of performance allows us to *borrow* the capacities of others in order to secure whatever it is we are entitled to.

I want to explain the idea of borrowed capacities more fully, but it is important, first, to be aware of its significance. We began, in Chapter IV, considering the possibility that the double standard of rights for children and adults was unjust. Those who would say that it is not must show a relevant difference between children and adults—relevant to granting rights to one group which are denied to the other. The difference most commonly cited is the difference in capacities. Although this difference does not correspond very precisely to the difference between children and adults, we conceded that the imprecision was not of overwhelming theoretical importance. However, we noticed that the differences in capacities seemed so relevant to the granting of rights primarily because of the assumption that a person must be able to initiate the exercise of a right on her or his own in order to have it. But this did not seem to me to be so. What is true is that a person who is incapable of initiating certain kinds of actions misses out on the joys of doing those things for herself. While there is undeniably joy in self-reliance, it does not provide life's only satisfactions. And a person who misses out on it should not also have to forfeit her rights, for she can still have those rights as long as she is in a position of demanding performance from others who do have the relevant capacities. So if children can borrow the capacities of those who have them, then the fact that some children do not have full capacities is not a relevant reason to impose a double standard of rights.

Borrowing the capacities of others is not at all unusual; we all do it at one time or another. None of us is so multi-talented that we can shape our lives without relying on the abilities and skills of others.[1] I would not defend myself in court or remove a growth from my leg. And it is not just that I do not have the time or the interest in doing so; I could not do either job because I am incapable. I do not have the training of a lawyer or a doctor; I do not have their experience or their skills. I have these capacities as potentials, I suppose, but it would take time and effort to develop them. In this respect, my position is quite analogous to the child's. And I certainly do not forfeit my rights to a lawyer or to medical attention because of my incapacity to attend to these things myself.

For some of our rights, the relative incapacities of children and adults are basically a matter of degree. Adults have the right to information about themselves which they may be incapable of understanding. Medical or psychiatric reports are most likely to fit into this category, but some financial information could be of this sort as well. When we cannot understand this information, we have the right to seek out someone—a doctor, a psychologist, an accountant, a knowledgeable friend —who can interpret it for us. Children have a similar problem —or they would if they had the right to access to information about themselves. They may well be incapable of understanding medical reports that find their way into a child's school file. But if this difference is one of degree, then the lack of capacity should not be used as an excuse to deny them the right to information, for children, too, could find someone who had the capacity to understand these things and make them accessible.

Another right in which the incapacities of children differ only in degree from those of adults is the right to vote. One commentator has suggested that the capacity required for that right is the capacity to "decide whether the candidates of one or the other major party are most likely to pursue the general policies which serve his interest."[2] What is necessary here is, on the one hand, a clear perception of your own interests. This would be your actual interests, and not what you may think your interests to be in some intuitive or uncritical way. On the other hand, in order to have this capacity you would have to have a pretty good sense of what the impact of various general policies would be if they were actually implemented. If we took this requirement seriously, I do not think anyone could honestly be said to possess this capacity. Leaving aside the fact that nobody seems to have the capacity to tell which candidates are likely to keep their campaign promises, we must still admit to precious little knowledge about how policies will work when put into practice. And what knowledge there is belongs to the "experts" in economics and government. These experts are more often than not in disagreement over technical points which the average and even the superior voter is incapable of understanding. Again, the problem is not simply a lack of information, or a lack of motivation to take the time to find out what is at issue. We do not have the intellectual tools to settle these debates—even to our own satisfaction. In this sense we are *incapable* of making an accurate judgment. What many of us end up doing at voting time is to take the word of some "expert" or another, second hand, from news analysts or political commentators. In short, we borrow their capacities to judge which candidates are pursuing which policies to what social ends. We are left on our own to decide which pursuits are in our own interests although, if the truth be known, that is a separate, highly abstract political question. So, although children understand relatively less than we adults of these matters, it is not quite so that we have a capacity which they lack when it comes to voting. We only rely a bit less on the capacities of others.

To be sure, with some other rights children would need to borrow capacities which most adults actually have. The rights related to running one's own financial affairs are rights which most adults are capable of exercising on their own. What I have in mind here are the rights to hold property, enter contracts, have an independent source of income (the right to work or receive welfare payments), receive credit, and have a bank account. In light of the economic organization of our society, this constellation of rights is necessary in order to maintain an independent financial existence. Such an existence is well within reach of most adults. The fact that they manage—for better or for worse—shows that they have the relevant capacities.

Many children are pretty clearly incapable of doing some of these things. A five-year-old could not manage a checkbook alone; a seven-year-old could probably not keep a budget or buy or sell a car without assistance. But this does not mean that these children could not make financial decisions. It means that they could not make them and carry them out on their own. There is no reason to think that they could not make these decisions with the help of a financial advisor. Such an advisor would have to be sufficiently adept at running the economic life of another and at doing so in such a way as to leave the major decisions in the client's hands. As a matter of fact, people of great wealth rely on such advisors all the time, and they do not forego their economic rights. There is no reason why children with financial advisors should have to forego theirs, either.

The point here is that by relying on the capacities of agents children could exercise their rights without doing harm to themselves or to others, without interfering with the obligations their parents or guardians might have to society at large, and without doing much damage to the system of rights and liberties. The role of the child's agent would be to supply information in terms which the child could understand, to make the consequences of the various courses of action a child might take clear to the child, and to do what is necessary to see that the right in question is actually exercised. A sensitive agent would try to do these things in such a way that the child could build on the experience and eventually act on her or his own. Any rights currently enjoyed by adults which children could exercise with the aid of agents are rights which children should have.

When I say that children should have these rights, I mean that all children should have them. I am not attempting to draw a new line fixing some lower age as the age of majority. As we saw in Chapter IV, drawing lines according to age is arbitrary, and drawing lines according to individual capacity is unwise at best and dangerous at worst. Strictly speaking, of course, children (and adults) who do not have the capacities even to use an agent do exhibit relevant differences from right holders. We might justifiably deny them rights on these grounds, but it is easier and safer not to do so. Very little is lost by granting children rights which they rarely claim. Nobody is obliged to claim their rights, and as a practical matter young children might rarely do so. In the typical cases we would expect that children below the age of six might well lack the combined skills and understanding necessary to recognize violations of right and to seek aid. ("Six" is only a rough guess here, figured from the age that children begin to learn and act on information from their peers.) But if children below this age are in a position to use an agent, there is no good reason to place barriers in their way. People should have their rights from birth.

Granting rights to all children is bound to raise the question of rights for fetuses, so something needs to be said about that issue here. This is actually a much less weighty question than it may seem on first consideration. In the first place, I am not arguing for children's rights on the grounds that they are entitled to them as human rights. Consequently, the issue of whether the fetus is a human person—a point of such contention in disputes about abortion—is not really relevant here. Any relevant difference between fetuses and children will do as a reason to treat these groups differently. Secondly, I am not discussing rights which have only to do with protection. Those rights are not granted on the basis of capacity anyhow. We may, if we wish, protect fetuses with a right to adequate nutrition, but if we do so it will be because we think that *fetuses* need this sort of protection—and not because we think that they are children.

The relevant differences between fetuses and children when it comes to granting rights are that children, and not fetuses, are members of society interacting with a variety of other people. The fetus in the womb experiences social life in such a limited and indirect way that it strains language to call it a social being. Beyond that, its range of possible experiences and its course of development are so limited until birth that we could not say that it needs certain options protected as rights in order to assure that its development takes a proper course later. Children, even in their first year, begin to make choices which affect their patterns of decision-making and future maturity. This can not be said of fetuses, so our concern for their well-being is not the same thing as concern for their rights. Our focus must be on the rights of children.

I realize that what I have suggested here is not likely to be met with much enthusiasm. Reticence and scepticism are more natural reactions to the idea that children should be entitled to the same rights which adults enjoy. These reservations need to be addressed, and I would like to discuss them under three headings. There are, first, the theoretical objections to a conception of rights which impose on others the obligations to serve children in particular ways. Second, there are the more practical objections concerning the difficulties of establishing effective relationships between children and their agents. Finally, in the next chapter, I shall consider some of the problems of implementation of a conception of child agents. If we can deal with these kinds of problems satisfactorily, then we should be in a position to acknowledge forthrightly the injustice of the double standard of rights.

One other sort of objection—the cost of a system of child agency—can be dismissed more quickly. In the first place, making something a right is partly a matter of giving it a status *beyond* cost analysis. Rights establish the basic relationships, and we should save money on the social luxuries first. But more to the point, if children do deserve these rights as a matter of social justice, then the cost must fall on everyone—not just them. If, for example, we decided that running elections has become too expensive, we would not seriously be willing to say that only those who now vote may continue to do so. The effect of that would be to treat new eighteen-year-olds unfairly. If voting *really* cost too much, we could hold elections less often. In fact, we are now prepared to have all new eighteen-year-olds vote despite consideration of cost. Those who are younger and ought to have this right too, should be treated similarly. The resistance to this notion reveals that the specter of the expense of children's rights is a way of reaffirming resistance to the social justice of children's rights. Of course, we are free to find the least expensive ways to implement child agency without undermining its effectiveness, but that is no objection to the idea of child agency. We can now turn to the theoretical problems with children's rights.

Our modern conception of rights as entitlements is, as we saw, designed primarily to help people have or do what they want even in the face of opposition or obstacles. To call something a right is to legitimize the desire for it and to discredit any opposition to someone's having it. But beyond entitlement there is another side to our conception of rights. This notion is usually expressed by saying that along with rights go certain responsibilities. People who say this do not mean that others have responsibilities to respect a person's rights. Rather, they mean that a person who has rights must also assume certain responsibilities in order to have the status of one who exercises rights. Just exactly what these responsibilities are should become clearer shortly, but it is fairly easy to see that in order to be the responsible person—that is, the person who is responsible for the consequences of her or his actions—one would have to have the capacities required to initiate the exercise of the right. This is so because we generally excuse people of the responsibility for their actions, morally and often legally, where it can be shown that they are incompetent in the relevant respects. Here we can find the source of an argument that certain capacities are relevant for the possession of certain rights. I want to develop this idea a bit in order to explain why I think we should reject it.

In the Anglo-American liberal tradition of political philosophy which has come down to us fairly well-intact since the seventeenth century, the concept of rights has played a rather important role. It is rights which are used to establish the boundaries of individual civil liberties. By the seventeenth century, political theorists were thinking of individual liberties in terms of what we today call "negative freedom:" "Negative freedom is the freedom to do what I want, to be unrestricted in the pursuit of my interests as I see them."[3] As another writer puts it: "By being free in this sense I mean not being interfered with by others. The wider the area of non-interference the wider my freedom."[4] One of the key functions of rights, as we saw in Chapter II, is to impose obligations of non-interference. Consequently, it is in terms of rights that we express and delimit our areas of negative freedom. I am, not speaking here of all of our rights, but primarily of our civil rights. These are rights which we have in our dealings with the state or in those areas where we, as a society, explicitly exclude state participation. The right to vote and the procedural rights of due process in court are examples of the first kind; the right to freedom of religious belief and expression is an example of the second.

Prior to the seventeenth century, a liberty was a privilege usually granted by a king to a favored person or group of people to have the use of some of the king's resources or to do something others were not permitted to do. For example, a king might grant someone the liberty of hunting in his forest or the liberty of a monopoly in the trade of salt in a certain part of the country. As privileges, liberties were granted at the king's pleasure and could be revoked by him should he wish to do so. Over the course of a couple of centuries, English kings gradually lost the power to grant or revoke certain liberties. That is, some liberties were established independently of the king's wishes and some, once established, could not be taken away. As these powers were gradually wrested from the king's hands, the concept of liberty took on its more modern meaning of negative freedom: non-interference in a person's activities by others—including the king.

Negative freedom was never completely unrestricted. It was never license to be left completely alone. Rather, certain aspects of life which had been subject to outside interference became private—at least with respect to the state. The English government was once able to prevent an accused person from being represented by a lawyer at a trial. After the right to counsel was established, the choice of having representation was left to the accused. Another way in which a person's civil liberties are restricted is by the civil liberties of others. In theory, if any one person's liberties were too extensive, it would allow them to interfere in the activities or with the property of others, and so diminish that other person's liberty. So each person's liberty must be regulated and balanced in light of the liberties of the rest. We can imagine liberties in a society as a system of spheres of mutual non-interference. At the center of each sphere is an individual member of society. The size of the sphere indicates the extent of that individual's liberty. Rights establish the surface boundaries of the spheres, and the system of rights prevents the spheres from penetrating one another. In the words of the influential legal philosopher H. L. A. Hart, ". . . it is I think a very important feature of a moral right that the possessor of it is conceived as having a moral justification for limiting the freedom of another . . ."[5] That is, my rights set boundaries on your freedom insofar as I may sometimes rightly tell you what or what not to do (with respect to me) in certain circumstances. For example, I may have the right to say "Leave me alone" or "Get off my land." By determining that others may or may not act toward me in a particular way, I reserve the prerogative of doing or having something for myself. Others, of course, may also determine how I shall act, so they can exercise a similar prerogative. Our interlocking system of negative freedoms defines the civil rights each of us has in society.

The negative freedom conception of civil rights requires a good deal from those who have them. Within it, to claim one's rights one must be able to exercise one's freedom. And this requires several well-developed capacities: sufficient intellect to understand one's place in the system of spheres, sufficient willpower to act within one's own sphere, the ability actually to make choices from within one's own range of alternatives. Each of these capacities demands a certain amount of skill from the person who has the rights, but more to the point here, they also demand an appreciation of one's place in society. To be a person who exercises rights, you should be prepared to act as a responsible member of an interlocking social order. Most of the people who hold this view of civil rights believe that there can only be significant civil liberty where the members of a society are aware of the mutually interdependent nature of the system of individual rights and accept its constraints (that is, assume responsibility for them).

As you might expect, the requirement that with rights go responsibilities is used to deny rights—and with them civil liberties—to children. John Stuart Mill makes the point emphatically in his essay "On Liberty." After insisting on the absolute right of the individual to freedom in those areas which concern no one but herself or himself, Mill goes on to remark:

It is, perhaps, hardly necessary to say that this doctrine is meant to apply only to human beings in the maturity of their faculties. We are not speaking of children, or of young persons below the age which the law may fix as that of manhood or womanhood. Those who are still in a state to require being taken care of by others, must be protected against their own actions as well as against external injury.[6]

By way of clarification Mill says that once people have the relevant capacities to use their liberty ("the capacity of being guided to their own improvement by conviction or persuasion"[7]), "compulsion . . . is no longer admissible as a means to their own good, and justifiable only for the security of others."[8] When people attain the level at which they can responsibly exercise their liberties, then they ought to have them. But for Mill, this does not generally happen in childhood.

The story, as I have told it so far, contains several reasons for denying certain rights to those without the relevant capacities, and it is time to single them out more explicitly. The passage quoted from Mill above mentions two. The first is that children might harm themselves if left to bump around in their own spheres. The second is that they might be harmed by others when their liberty brings them up against situations for which they are not adequately prepared. These are the concerns of paternalism, "the interference with a person's liberty of action justified by reasons referring exclusively to the welfare, good, happiness, needs, interests or values of the person being coerced."[9] We can see how paternalism works if we imagine how it would be used to deny a child the right to choose an alternative home environment. (As adults, we are not required by the state to live in any particular place or with any particular group of people.)

Suppose that a child is quite unhappy at home and wishes to live elsewhere. We can imagine that the child is approximately twelve years old, that the parents have done nothing which could legally be described as child abuse or neglect, that they have genuine concern for the child's development, and that they are rather strict disciplinarians. Let us also imagine that the child can stay with the parents of a friend, but it is by no means clear that the arrangement would be permanent. Should the child have the right to choose to leave home? The paternalist would say "no," and offer two kinds of reasons. In the first place, the child may have needs that she or he is not really aware of. Goldstein, Freud, and Solnit, in their book *Beyond the Best Interest of the Child*, claim that one of the overriding needs of childhood is continuity of a parent-figure. Their motto is "leave things as they are unless you can prove that some alternative will be less detrimental to the child." The child may be unhappy, but the child cannot know of the future unhappiness which the lack of continuity at this stage of her or his life would cause. Thus, the child should be coerced into remaining at home in the name of his or her own good.

The other version of the paternalist argument is that the child in this example could be quite incapable of recognizing whether an alternative home would be better or worse than the present one. It is quite possible that the child could get into a situation of serious physical or emotional abuse. Owing to the child's lack of experience of the real horrors of an unhappy home and the child's presumed inability to put long-term interests ahead of present displeasures, it is necessary to sacrifice the child's liberty to her or his welfare, good, happiness, and so on. The right to an alternative home environment is too dangerous to be left to the child on this view.

There are other ways in which children's lack of capacities are used to deny them rights. One we encountered in John Locke's exposition of the child-protection ideology in Chapter I. Locke argued that parents have an obligation to God to protect their children. We may prefer to think of the obligation as one we have to our society for the development of its future members. In any event, child-rearing is not exclusively a private matter. If parents do have obligations to the society at large, they may not let their children do anything which would cause them to fail to discharge *their own* obligations. Suppose the parents of the twelve-year-old in our example do have an obligation to raise a productive member of society if they decide to have children. Then they can be held responsible for failures of child-rearing. If the parents of the child's friend do not do an adequate job, the responsibility is not theirs, since the biological parents should not have relinquished supervision in the first place. The upshot of this is that the child should not have a right to an alternative home environment since that right could interfere with the discharge of prior parental obligations.

A fourth reason for denying the right to those without the relevant capacities is that granting it to them would be frivolous to the point of making a mockery out of the very idea of rights. This is a little hard to see in the case of a twelve-year-old, but if the right to an alternative home environment is to belong to all children, it becomes quite clear. A one- or two-year-old child barely has a notion of what a home environment is, let alone a concept of "alternatives." In order to actually exercise the right in a meaningful way, the child would have to be able to assess the relative merits of the alternatives, perceive her or his own proper interests, and act on the basis of that understanding. Anything short of this is not a significant exercise of a right— and the two-year-old child falls considerably short of being able to do this owing to her or his lack of the relevant capacities. Since the child cannot really do anything with the right, it is pointless to bestow it. And given the seriousness with which we generally treat our rights in this society, extending rights in these situations can only serve to degrade the concept of rights rather than to enhance the status of children.

A final reason for denying this right to children is that in the course of exercising it they could do inadvertent harm to others. I am not speaking here of the harm that would come from acting beyond the limit of the right; anyone, not just children, can abuse his rights. But there are situations falling short of interference with the rights of others in which we may prevent them from doing things they want to do, or in which we cause them to do things which put them out a little. Often it is possible to exercise our rights in ways which lead to minimal disruptions in the lives of others or to exercise them in more intrusive ways. People who recognize the difference and are sensitive to the system try to do as little disrupting as possible. But children who do not have the capacity to see that there are ways and there are ways not to exercise their rights will, as often as not, cause more havoc than is necessary. The system of negative freedoms is sufficiently delicate that it needs a large dose of mutual good will to work really well (to maintain a large area of civil liberty). To admit people to it who do not have the capacities to use their rights as considerately as possible is unnecessarily to jeopardize the system. The child who is changing home environments may not realize the extent of the imposition on her or his friend's parents. They may be willing to put up with a certain amount so as to see that the child does not go rightless in this case, but unless the child is aware of this and treats them accordingly, this sort of alternative home arrangement could come under attack and ultimately limit the options available to others who would exercise this right. In order to protect the right, one could argue that it should be denied to children.

Each of these arguments depends for its plausibility on the assumption of the impenetrability of the sphere of negative freedom. (The third argument is a bit different from the others, but it assumes this as well.) What I mean by this is that in each case we are presented with a cut-and-dried choice: the child is either left strictly alone to make a decision or the child has no right. But as soon as we entertain a third option—that the child exercise the right by borrowing the capacities of an agent who is specifically obligated to help—these arguments lose most of their force. An agent could certainly inform the child of the advantages and the importance of continuity, just as the agent could see whether the proposed alternative home was likely to be better or worse than the child's present one. While it is true that an agent, as I understand the term, could not absolutely prevent a child from making a particular choice which rested within the rightful range, this possibility should not be blown out of proportion. Agents would be trusted advisors, and their views are likely to be respected by children. Furthermore, we are speaking of children who are at least old enough to articulate the desire to change homes, and so are presumably old enough to comprehend something of what would be involved in the move—as long as the agent expressed the situation in an appropriate way (i.e., at the child's level).

In a similar vein, there is no very good reason to think that children would not be able to exercise this right meaningfully once we have specified an adult whose obligation it is to assess the relative merits of the child's alternatives, to help the child articulate his or her proper interests, and to lay the groundwork for the child's subsequent action. Far from being frivolous, extending this right to children is likely to have a significant impact on parent-child relationships to the extent that children will be in a position to make good on the threat to leave home. Likewise the agent would be experienced enough and knowledgeable enough to see that the changes of residence which do occur do so with a minimal amount of fuss and inconvenience. The sort of diplomacy required here is well within the reach of most people, and we can suppose that agents would be sensitive to it. But even if particular agents are not very smooth about helping out their clients, it would be unfair to paint them as less effective than the average adult would be in exercising a similar right—and that is all I really want to insist on. Finally, there is the matter of parental responsibility. While it is true that parents would be irresponsible to society informally to abandon their children to someone else, under a system of agents there would be formalized and traceable transfers of responsibility. Guardianship, after all, is not an unknown phenomenon in our society, and rights can and do have binding force in law. In sum, all of the arguments for withholding civil rights from those who lack the relevant capacities are remarkably short-sighted about the kinds of support which might be offered to the potential right holders instead.

Actually, this is quite understandable from the perspective of the theory of negative freedom. On this view liberties are believed to have intrinsic value. That means we value them not only for what they can get us, but also because we think it is important to make our own choices and do things for ourselves. When we insist on non-interference, it is not only because we do not want others to *prevent* us from having or doing what we will. Even if they were entirely helpful, we might object that we were being denied the opportunity to exercise our freedom. It would be maddening and stifling to have someone sense your every desire and satisfy it before you could do so yourself. It would also be an interference with your liberty.

Although the exercise of freedom is intrinsically valuable, we do not just go around making choices for the pure joy of it. These choices will allow us to have or do things which contribute to our happiness, welfare, well-being, and so on. Civil liberties are also, in that respect, an instrument for attaining some of these goods. But they are not the only instruments. No doubt it would be wonderful if we could be the architects of our own happiness, welfare, and well-being. But we cannot always do that. And when we cannot, we need not despair. It is far better to call on others to help than to go without. When rights impose only or primarily obligations of non-interference on others, they allow us the maximum exercise of our own powers—what we might call individual self-determination. These are the sort of rights which are most closely associated with negative freedom and civil liberty in our political and legal traditions. To have freedom of religion, for example, means that each person chooses the form of his or her own spiritual life (if any). We cannot say that people without this freedom will not have satisfying spiritual lives. That is belied by the innumerable people who were content in their religion at times and in places where belief was dictated by the state. But when we make religious freedom a liberty, we imply that there is a further satisfaction in establishing one's own spiritual life on one's own. And this may be so, but it is a long way from suggesting that religion must be freely chosen or done without.

If we agree that some children some of the time—or even many children most of the time—do not have the capacities to exercise these civil liberties, we are still a long way from making them go rightless. For rights can impose obligations of performance as well as obligations of non-interference. In other words, rights can be used not only to stake out our areas of negative freedom, they can also be used to require others to help us to secure those things which we need for our happiness, welfare, or well-being. Rights which impose obligations of performance allow us in effect to borrow the capacities of others to secure whatever it is that we are entitled to. Theoretically, there is no barrier here; we need only broaden our view.

As a practical matter, however, we need some sense of whether children could effectively use agents in the exercise of their civil rights. For if children did not have the capacity to use an agent, the differences between them and adults would be relevant to the maintenance of the double standard.

In order to deal with this problem, we need to divide children into three groups: those who could use agents effectively, those who are incapable of taking and following advice, and those who do not even know how to claim their rights. The first group poses no problem, and neither does the third. Children who are unable to claim their rights will not get what they are entitled to. That may be too bad in some cases, but it would be inaccurate to say that these children are rightless. The difference here is not merely semantic. We are, correctly, reluctant to say that a right has been violated in the absence of some indication that the person in question tried to claim it. To have a right to something does not mean that you are required to do or have it; it means that you are entitled to it if you claim it. When a person makes no claim, nobody else is put in the position of interfering or failing to do what they are obligated to do. The claim sets the obligations in motion. There is an exception to this. When people work actively to keep others ignorant of their rights and so prevent them from making their claims, we feel that they have violated the rights of others. But the case we are discussing is not like that. These children are imagined to be very young—say under four years of age—and not developed enough to even make the kinds of claims we are referring to here. All we need to say in these cases is that when these children are developed enough to make their claims, they will be entitled to do so. That is why the difference is not semantic. They have their rights all along; the rights are simply waiting to be used.

The difficult case is the one of children presumed incapable of taking and following advice. As we noticed earlier, Mill suggested that the problem with children is that they lack the capacity "of being guided to their own improvement by conviction and persuasion." This is certainly not true of most children (and it was probably not true of Mill) but it may well be true of a substantial enough number of children often enough to pose a problem. So let us assume that there will be times when children will be incapable of using an agent properly. The first thing to notice is that even when this is true, the harm to *others* would be minimal. We are not talking about children being able to do whatever they please. Each child's rights are circumscribed by the rights of others. The child may have better or worse options, but all the options fall within a range limited by what is socially acceptable. We may not like to see our children vote for candidates from crackpot political parties or spend their money in ways we think of as foolish or work instead of going to school, but by making these rights available to adults, we have already indicated that the fabric of society will not be ripped apart should anyone pursue these options. If we really thought it would be, we would have foreclosed them. And in some cases we have.

The next thing to notice is that under a system of child's agents someone would be aware of the course of action the child was about to take, and be in a position to cushion any resulting shocks. An agent would presumably know or suspect that her advice was not being well-received, or was being received by someone who had no intention of following it. And though the agent could not rightfully prevent the child from exercising the right in question, the consequences of the child's action, should they be bad, would at least not be a surprise.

There is, finally, something to be said for learning from experience. It does not just strike us one day that the advice of others can be helpful and worth following. The more usual story is that sometimes we ignore it and wish we had not, and sometimes we follow it and are glad we did. Slowly, and through practice, we come to develop the capacities which free us of the need to do so in some aspects of our lives. The fact that a child is incapable of taking and following advice at some moments in her or his life does not betray a permanent character flaw. The child is not to be condemned forever rightless, or even left to acquire the relevant capacity by chance. A sure route to the maturity of the faculties Mill valued so highly is the monitored aid in actually exercising one's rights: hands-on training.

So far as I can see, the differences in capacities between children and adults are not very important when it comes to having rights. There will be differences, to be sure, in how these respective groups *exercise* their rights. Fewer adults and more children will need agents in order to compensate for their own lack of capacities. But the use of agents is not unheard of in our society. Large numbers of people are employed in this way: lawyers, stock brokers, insurance and real estate salespersons—to name only the most obvious examples. Whether we could have a useful system of agents for children is another question—and a crucial one. For if the system could not work, the differences in capacities would actually be relevant to the having of rights. Equal rights for children will depend upon the workability of a system of children's agents.

CHAPTER VI

Child Agents

We are now at the point of having developed an alternative to the caretaker ideology—a new perspective from which to work out a system of children's rights. There are several important advantages to this alternative. First, it provides an insight into the limitations of the caretaker ideology. We saw how the emphasis on child protection tended to obscure the fact that we are really not that clear about what actually is in the child's best interest, to gloss over the potential conflicts of interest between children and their caretakers, and to ignore the abilities of children by focusing on questions of *which* adult should have control. The second important advantage is that it gives us a clear understanding of what rights are and how they are used. On this conception rights define social relationships by entitling people to do or have one thing or another. They do this by obligating others not to interfere with our activities, or obligating some of them to aid us in doing or having something. By saying that we have a right to some relationship with the rest of society, we indicate its importance and also the possibility that others may wish to keep us from it. Consequently, the concept of a right is typically invoked to conserve a relationship under attack or to justify a movement for social change which attempts to define new relationships. The second use is the one which is of relevance to children's rights. The third advantage of this perspective is that it offers an account of the injustice of the double standard of rights for children and adults. In order

to justify the double standard, one would need to find a difference between children as a group and adults as a group which
was relevant to withholding rights from the first which were
granted to the second. As we noted, a difference in capacities is
typically supposed to do this. However, the concept of *borrowed
capacities* makes this difference substantially irrelevant—as long
as we can work out a system which effectively imposes obligations of performance on those with the relevant capacities to
those children who have need of them. Thus, the final element
in our alternative ideology is a conception of what it would
take to grant children the same rights which adults presently
enjoy: a system of child agents. The task of the agent is not
to protect the child, but rather to provide those capacities which
would be necessary in order for the child to exercise her or his
rights.

In the previous chapter, I alluded to the fact that the implementation of a system of child agents may prove to be a difficult task. And should it prove to be so difficult as to approach
impossibility, then my argument against the double standard
of rights will not be very persuasive. So the practical question
needs to be faced here: who would be the child's agent?

There is a great temptation, having developed this perspective, to apply it to the task of drawing up a blueprint for social
change, complete with a system of agents and worked out to the
last detail. That is a temptation I plan to resist here. The problem with blueprints is that libraries are full of them. They make
fine reading, but in two weeks they are back on the shelf collecting dust. When confronted with a fully-developed alternative
to our present practices, people usually react in one of three
ways: They dismiss it as utopian idealism; they are intrigued,
but see no way to move from where we are to where we want
to be; or they see the transitional steps too well and despair of
ever making such a substantial change in our social structure.

As none of these reactions seems very appealing, I offer no
blueprint. I prefer to think of this child agency ideology as
offering a vantage point from which we may assess develop-
ments and changes in our relationships to children. In other
words, we can use it to decide whether any specific proposal
concerning our relations with children is or is not progressive

in the sense that it moves beyond caretaking in the direction of establishing equal rights for children. We can use it for *any* proposal from one concerning the way decisions are made within a particular family to how time shall be spent in a day care center, to federal or state legislation affecting children. The vantage point will help us to see the ways in which our present efforts fall short of our goals, and it should give us some direction as to what we might do to change things for the better. We make these evaluations all the time, anyway, so there is no reason to think that a more sharply defined or more satisfactorily-grounded perspective will suddenly require us to take on large-scale social architecture. Nobody should feel that they have to refuse the conception of children's rights developed here because there is too much work to be done.

I want now to clarify what it means to see things from the child agency perspective by describing how, in answering a series of five questions, a person might use it. These are:

1. How would we treat an adult in this situation?
2. What capacities do we assume that an adult uses in order to exercise her or his rights here?
3. Can we presume that the child (children) in question lack(s) these capacities?
4. Are these the sort of capacities which can be borrowed?
5. Is there an available agent who could donate the use of her or his capacities?

Suppose that we wanted to evaluate a child's rights to confidentiality of information. For the most part, it is standard practice to deny children control over materials about them such as the reports of doctors or hospitals and the files their schools keep on them. More specifically, children are denied access to medical or educational records without parental permission, and secondly, parents have access to that information along with the right to disseminate it without obtaining the child's permission. It is this second point, having to do with confidentiality, which we are going to focus on here. Should children have the right to prevent their parents (or anyone else) from obtaining their personal medical or educational records? Should they have the right to prevent their parents from divulging that information to others? Let us see if we can answer these questions by working through the five listed above.

Adults are routinely given information about themselves when they request it. Hospitals and schools may sometimes balk at doing this, but they can generally be forced to turn over their files through a court order. Furthermore, confidential information may only be divulged by these institutions or agencies when the adult who is the subject of the information specifically gives permission to release it. There is no other adult with the appointed task of deciding whether information may be divulged to others despite the wishes of the subject. The only major exceptions to this are adults who have been declared incompetent in a legal proceeding. Then they are treated as typical children. That is, control of the information is left in the hands of another. But the reality for most adults is that others can have access to their files only when they consent to give it. I am, of course, ignoring information leaks and spills as well as information illegally obtained or gotten through great pressure on the "consenting" adult. There are plenty of problems with making confidentiality effective—but these are not our concerns here. We are now looking at the principle of confidentiality to see whether it ought to apply to children as it does to adults.

What capacities do we assume that an adult uses in order to exercise her or his right to confidentiality? Two come to mind. The first is the capacity to understand the information contained in the records. Actually, an adult would not need to be able to understand it in its raw form, but merely be capable of understanding a faithful interpretation of it. Even for adults, the right to information entitles them to more than mere noninterference with their access to it. They are also entitled to find someone to explain it to them, though perhaps for a fee. Still, the capacity to understand the (interpreted) information is not by itself sufficient to exercise the right to confidentiality. An adult is also presumed capable of making reasonably accurate judgments about the consequences of letting out some information or withholding it. For example, would I be better or worse off for granting a prospective employer the right of general access to my medical records? This can often be a complex and delicate judgment. To be able to make it, a person would need to assess the importance of the information to the employer, the customary practices in this area, the extent of the damage that a questionable health record would have on employment chances, and the impact of a refusal on the employer's perception of the potential employee. These considerations only scratch the surface, and a person who was truly capable of making such a judgment would probably need a good deal of experience to do it well.

Can we presume that the child (children) in question lack(s) these capacities? This, of course, depends to a large extent on the nature of the information and who wants it. The capacity to understand interpreted information probably comes sooner than the capacity to make judgments about the consequences of disclosing that information to others. Nevertheless, there are surely times when the judgment will be easy—well within the range of the capacities of many children. Difficult judgments may be beyond the capacities of many adults. But by and large, the capacity to make judgments about the consequences of disclosure of information is developed through experience, so we can assume that at some time or another nobody has it. And surely most children do not have the opportunity to develop it early in life. On balance, we should presume that children do not have the second capacity unless and until we have reason to believe otherwise.

Are these the sorts of capacities which can be borrowed? We rely on the understanding and judgments of others all the time—*whenever* advice is given. From the perspective of the giver, there is no problem about putting these capacities at the service of others. Judging the consequences of a person's actions may be a special skill, but it is not private in the sense that we can each do it only for ourselves. Of course, we can do it for others—the more relevant question is whether the recipient can accept the advice. That is, is the recipient the sort of person who is capable of using the understanding and judgment of another? This is more relevant because the capacity to take advice is not the sort which can be borrowed.

We have already touched on this point in Chapter V. Some people (primarily children) are not capable of taking advice.

Although this number may be relatively small, those who have this incapacity are relevantly different from everyone else when it comes to the case for equal rights. Nevertheless, there are reasons for giving them advice anyhow; for one thing, they may learn from the experience. So with this qualification duly noted, we may say that the capacities of understanding and judging the effect of disclosing confidential information can be borrowed.

Is there an available agent who could donate the use of her or his capacities? Not just anyone will do. We are speaking of putting someone under an obligation of performance—and obligations are serious business. The proper agent will have to meet several conditions. First, the agent must actually have the capacities in question. But this is only the beginning. We ought not impose this sort of obligation on anyone who would suffer an undue hardship when discharging it. To put someone at the service of another in such a way that the donor lost a job, deteriorated in health, or suffered an extended separation from family and friends would be grossly unfair.

Furthermore, the agent must not have a conflict of interest with the child over the possible use of the information. This is the main reason why we should not be too quick to think of the agent as one of the child's parents. Imagine a situation in which the child has a poor health record. It is possible that in a custody hearing for guardianship of the child such a record could be used by one parent to build a case that the child was neglected by the other parent. While the divulgence of this information would be in the interest of the first parent, it is not so clear that it is in the interest of the child. Here the parent would not be an appropriate agent—no matter how well refined her or his capacities.

The child must also trust the agent. Donating capacities is meaningless to a person who cannot or will not accept their use. The donor must be more than capable; she or he must be acceptable to the child in need of an agent. It may, at times, be impossible to find an acceptable agent for a sufficiently suspicious child, but if the system is going to break down here we should at least have made a good faith effort. In other words, the child should have more than one or two choices.

Finally, the agent must literally be available: reachable when needed. There is no sense to obligating someone who is nowhere to be found or too busy when the decision about whether to release some information must be made. It often happens that these decisions cannot wait, or that the consulation is most effective when it takes place face to face. So if the child agent system is to work, we must be willing to make it convenient. The possibility of equal rights for children is only as real as the mechanisms are workable. A system that does not bring children into close contact with their agents will have the effect of making the differences in capacity between children and adults more significant, thus providing justification for a double standard.

We have gone at last to the practical question: Who will be the child's agent? Who has the relevant capacities, the time, energy and resources, the proper interests, the trustworthiness, and the availability to undertake obligations of performance on behalf of the child? It is hard to imagine that any one person could fill this bill for all of the rights a given child might be entitled to exercise. Thus, we should not expect to designate an agent for each child at birth the way some people designate godparents. This would have the effect of making children's rights largely ceremonial. But if Aunt Jane is not to be my child's agent, how many agents is she to have, and how are they to be employed?

Some useful models for thinking about this problem are the laws of many European countries which impose a duty to come to the aid of people in distress—the Good Samaritan laws, as they are called. People in Eastern Europe, in the Scandinavian countries, in France, and in West Germany who have been in accidents or are otherwise in danger have a right to rescue. The obligations imposed on others by this right naturally go way beyond non-interference. Someone must take positive steps to do something. But who? The various Good Samaritan laws try to specify this *situationally*. The person meeting certain characteristics who finds herself or himself in a situation where aid is needed is obligated to give it. Being the right person in the right place at the right time makes you the "someone" in: "If a person has a right to something, then someone has an obligation to help that person have or do that thing."

European Good Samaritan laws differ from country to country about who has the duty to rescue and when. There is a good summary for the interested reader in Aleksander W. Rudzinski, "The Duty to Rescue: A Comparative Analysis." As he points out, in some countries the duty is imposed only on witnesses to a person in distress, while in others everyone informed of the danger has an obligation to do something about it. What one is obligated to do is, of course, the crucial question. Sometimes a person is obligated to take direct action—but this obligation is limited by the witness's capacity to perform such action under the circumstances. A person with a heart condition is not obligated to jump into a river to save a drowning victim. Some laws obligate a person to obtain help for the person in trouble; others obligate the person to notify some proper authority.[1] There are countless variations on the possible ways of working these laws. The point to bear in mind, however, is that it is quite possible to draft a law which specifies rights by imposing obligations on specific but unnamed persons. One should not reject the notion of child agents on the grounds that it would be difficult to put the rights in question into words.

Still, the parallel to child agency is not exact. We do not want the first able warm body that comes along to do the job. We are not as fussy about our rescuers as we are about our agents. But this is not a substantial difference; it only requires that we build some choice for the child into the model. A person who is otherwise fit for the job might be disqualified if the child did not want that particular agent.

We have already said that a child's agent must have certain capacities: time, energy, and resources, the proper interests, trustworthiness, and availability. But it is not easy to specify these with greater precision. That is not because there is an essential vagueness in each of these terms (although there is some), but rather because precision here raises a raft of touchy issues about how the policy of creating child agents should be handled. These issues are touchy because they are important, strongly contested, and without prospect of immediate solution. They include:

Should child agents be professionals?
Should they be paid, and by whom?
To whom shall the child agent be accountable for the quality of her or his work?
What is the relationship of the child agent to the child's family?

These issues are interlocking in the sense that certain answers to some of them dispose us toward particular answers to others. Furthermore, they are issues which come up in all social service endeavors. They are not peculiar to *child* agency. But this does not make them any less touchy. I cannot solve them here. In fact, it would be foolish to settle them without experimenting a little. These are only partly questions of principle. Where a solution would run deeply against our collective grain, we need not try it out. But mostly these are questions about what would work effectively—and there we cannot say without a pilot project or two. What we can do is speculate about which pilot project to try out first. That is the most we should expect from a discussion of these issues at present; that and a sense that there is something here worth trying.

Should Child Agents Be Professionals?

"Professional agents" conjures an image of massive and expansive bureaucracy. While it is important not to make people's rights depend upon inconvenience or cost to others, this only works up to a point. We are, after all, thinking about this problem in terms of social justice, and the burden of another bureaucracy could well overwhelm the importance of children's rights. In light of this, we need to be especially cautious about creating a class of professional child agents. But even if we could afford professionals here, there are a number of good reasons to avoid them.

One of the biggest dangers is that professionalism would limit the number of agents available to children and make their services scarce. If agents had to be certified, and the demand for them was very great, it is entirely possible that child agency would go the way of probation. There is nothing wrong with the *concept* of probationary supervision as an alternative to jail. Yet it is commonly conceded that large caseloads make a mockery of the concept. A probation officer may be as well-trained and as skilled as you please, but seeing a client once each month for an hour or so affords no opportunity for the use of those skills. The scarcity of the resource undermines the advantages of professionalism.

Problems created by a limited number of agents would be compounded in dealing with children's rights. Clients cannot be scheduled. We do not exercise our rights at regular intervals, but rather when the need or the opportunity arises. The agent must be available then. An appointment two weeks later may well be too late. A student might need information to contest a suspension from school, and it is entirely possible that the suspension period would be over by the time a busy agent took on the case. Some non-professional, interested adult might well have been able to do that particular job in short order with minimal difficulty. To insist on professionals in cases like this could complicate matters hopelessly.

A related difficulty is that professionalism typically carries bureaucracy along with it, and bureaucracy itself would be a problem here. With bureaucracy comes the danger of hardening of the institutional arteries. Presently, many of our rights require a certain amount of red tape in order to be exercised. One must register to vote, serve notice to cancel a consumer contract, apply for information, and so on. This is part of the reason why children need agents in the first place: procedures can act as barriers to the uninitiated. If child agents were bureaucratized, we could expect that there would be a layer of red tape and forms-in-triplicate between children and their agents. The effect of this might easily be to put children off and discourage them from seeking an agent in the first place. Again, the loss of access tends to undermine the advantages of skill and quality. We need agents, but not agencies.

I want to mention a third problem with professionalism which is more speculative. It is not a problem with professionalism *per se*, but with professionalism in the social services at this time in our history. Although the caretaker ideology—as I have outlined it in Chapter I—has come in for serious criticism recently, it is still the predominant vantage point for dealing with the place of children in our society. Our present institutions which deal with children have been designed with protection in mind. If professional child-agents are trained in these institutions, they may have great difficulty distinguishing child agency from caretaking. But even if we could somehow see to it that the training of child agents kept this difference clear, the institutionalization of child agency would have to take place outside of the framework of the older caretaker services. Otherwise, we would end up with new institutions in name only. One way to try to deal with this danger is to cut the new institutions off entirely from the old—and one way to do that is to reject professionalism and bureaucracy for much more informal arrangements.

I do not wish to minimize either the abilities of professionals or the advantages of professionalism here. There are benefits to be derived from trained agents, and the case for professionals rests on two of them. The first is that special skills require special talents; the second, that quality control is important when we are dealing with important decisions. Do child agents need special skills? That depends upon which skills we are talking about. Most of the rights which adults have do not require special skills in order to be exercised—at least the holder of the right is not assumed to have any special skills. Adults have the right to be represented by a lawyer in criminal proceedings. By no stretch of the imagination does this mean that adults must have lawyers' skills. The standard abilities required to function in society are about all that is needed to exercise rights to vote, obtain credit, seek information about ourselves, and the like. These are not special skills, either. Since these are the kinds of skills which would be loaned to children in need of them, they cannot be the basis for a profession of child agency, either. The child operating on borrowed capacities need not be in a substantially better position than the typical adult when it comes to exercising rights.

There are, nevertheless, skills which an agent must possess which the typical adult does not need in order to exercise her or his rights. These are the skills of interpreting information to children, making their choices clear to them, explaining the consequences of various courses of action, demonstrating that they are to be trusted, and carrying out the aims of another.

These are, no doubt, special skills. They require sensitivity informed by knowledge of child development on the one hand, and the discipline to separate one's own perspective from that of the child-client on the other. We can well believe that some training in these matters would make agents substantially more effective.

The other main consideration for professional child agents is quality control over the process. A child with an inept agent is a child without rights. This problem is particularly acute for children precisely because they are in need of agents. Most adults who use an agent for one purpose or another have some idea of the quality of service they are receiving. I may not be capable of doing a doctor's work, but I can usually recognize a bad job. But children who need agents may well lack the understanding and the experience to assess the quality of the work that is being done for them. Since it is not very realistic to expect that children can be made more critical in this respect, the best remedy would be to examine the skills of potential agents in advance, and to certify them. In this way, people who were hopelessly bad at the job would be barred from serving as agents.

Agent skill and quality do need to be concerns if we expect children to have equal rights in fact as well as on paper. Yet, we should not worry too much that these skills will be absent if we avoid the full-scale professional agent and agency model. As a practical matter, people who are presently involved in child services will be called upon to fill the role of agent at one time or another. Besides parents, they are adults who are in the closest contact with children. They are the adults who will be most available to be called upon by children with rights to exercise when, for one reason or another, a parent would be inappropriate. Still, although children will need to draw on their resources, they should have no monopoly on these jobs, and we should not presume that they are necessarily the most qualified to be agents. In any event, child services are not distributed uniformly throughout our society, and many children simply do not come into contact with "professionals" on a regular basis. That is reason enough to spread the work more widely.

On balance, it seems to me that it would be best to avoid certifying agents unless other arrangements fail hopelessly. I suspect that the dangers of a more informed system would be minimal because, in fact, the people who are most likely to take on the job will have related skills and training. Teachers, social workers, day care workers, public health nurses, youth workers, Big Brothers and Sisters, and so on, have the skills of a child agent to a great extent. What they would need is a commitment to being agents rather than caretakers. Some of them have this, too. Others will have to be convinced. In any event, as long as the caretakers do not have a monopoly on child agency, there will be space to push for the child agent perspective. If we avoid certification, non-professionals committed to that perspective will be able to help children exercise their rights. This may not be as well-organized a system as we would like, but it is probably the best we could hope for under the circumstances.

Should Child Agents Be Paid, and By Whom?

This issue is tied fairly directly to the question of professionalism. Professional agents would obviously have to be paid, and that would pretty much guarantee the vast and expansive bureaucracy which makes equal rights for children seem so impractical. But if we must avoid payment in order to avoid officialdom, then we can not expect that many people will be able to take on child agency as a full-time job. The lack of compensation for agents could lead to a number of difficulties. In the first place, unpaid child agents would most often turn out to be interested adults; that is, adults who had a particular interest in a certain child or a specific situation. If every child could count on such an adult, that might not be so bad. But we should not assume that every child can. Indeed, the children who cannot might well be the ones who would need agents the most. Just because they have no one to rely on, their rights are in serious jeopardy. So a system of unpaid agents might not be the most efficient way to distribute agents where they are needed most.

Another problem with using unpaid agents is that it would

be very difficult to enforce the obligations of performance. How could we push an agent to do her or his job if that became necessary? Loss of the job is no threat, and shame will only work up to a point. We might attach civil penalties to the failure to perform an agent's obligations, and let the child sue for damages. But the child would need an agent to get to court. How easy would it be to find an agent to bring another agent to court?

Despite the difficulties, unpaid agency makes the most sense as an initial approach to the practical problems. On the one hand there is not likely to be much money around for this social experiment in the foreseeable future and, on the other, there is little reason to believe that money would make the system work. Our experience with public payment for social services of this sort comes primarily from the funding of legal services for the poor.

We might anticipate that the dangers of public funding of child agents would be similar to the problems of public funding of lawyers. There is, first, the matter of the heavy caseload. Since the public inevitably does not fund enough defenders, each of them is short on time and resources with which to do an adequate job. Every client is shortchanged a little—and some are shortchanged more than that. The size of the caseload also makes it difficult for the lawyer to take a personal interest in any given case. The client comes and goes, and will probably see a different lawyer next time anyway. Furthermore, if the lawyer is salaried or if the fee is standardized, there is little incentive to aspire beyond mediocrity. These lawyers really cannot do a good job, and when they realize this, it is easy to become cynical and not to try. Finally, public defenders have stronger ties to the people they see in court every day—judges and prosecuting attorneys—than they do to their clients (whom they barely know). As a result, it is not clear for whom they are actually working. These problems are well documented, for the system of public defenders has been rather thoroughly studied. It is not easy to see how a system of public payment child agents would fare much better.

An intermediate solution here might be to fund recruiters and trainers of child agents. It is pretty clear that some people would have to devote quantities of time and energy to the shaping and securing of new institutions, but this energy need not take the form of direct service. Paid professionals creating networks of unpaid agents could be a manageable and relatively inexpensive way to extend and entrench the use of child agents in our society. It is not really possible to tell in advance whether a plan of this sort would be effective, but at least it is neither *clearly* too expensive nor *clearly* to haphazard to justify rejecting equal rights for children.

To Whom Shall the Child Agent be Accountable for the Quality of Her or His Work?

Ultimately there are only two choices here: the agent is either accountable to the child/client or to a supervisor who has the responsibility of setting and enforcing standards. If the agent is directly responsible to the child, there is less of a chance that a conflict of interest will arise between them. The point here is not so much that the child can command the loyalty of the agent as that the agent can pursue the child's interest without the restraint of having to answer to some other person as well. An agent who was accountable to more than one person would constantly be in the position of having to reconcile or compromise the interests of two masters—should they disagree with one another. Moreover, the agent would have her or his own interest in concealing this conflict from the child in order to minimize the difficulty of the job, but this points to a much more general problem about making the agent accountable solely to the child.

Children who need agents may often not possess the capacities required to evaluate the quality of the agent's work. They may have neither the understanding nor the experience to tell whether someone could do a better job in helping them to exercise their rights. In situations like this, the agent is accountable to a person who is unable to hold her or him to account. In other words, there is no accountability, only good will. We might decide that we will just have to trust the competence and good will of our agents in these cases, or we could put child agents under supervision.

Once we have supervisors for agents, we have the makings of a bureaucracy. The more strict we are about accountability, the more centralized the organization which does the supervision will have to be. Presumably there will be a large number of child agents, and they will have to report on what they are doing or be observed in action. A small number of supervisors would need a large support staff, and a large number of supervisors would need a coordinating organization to maintain uniformity of standards. Either way, bureaucracy wins. We would have to create an ongoing organization complete with its own institutional needs and interests.

Agencies like the one we are imagining here have a way of making demands on their personnel which are not always the demands of their clients. For example, suppose that some children are not satisfied with the standards which the agency uses to evaluate its agents. These children might begin to agitate for a change and cause embarrassment, inconvenience, or even trouble for the agency. What role is the agent to play in all this? On the one hand, it is the job of the agent to loan the capacities which children need to exercise their rights. Perhaps an agent should help the child to plan a demonstration. Yet the agent is, on the other hand, paid by the agency and judged on the basis of its current standards. Agitation for change could place the agent's job in jeopardy. This kind of conflict may not arise every day, but the agent in this kind of set-up is always potentially in the middle when clients are not happy about what is being done for them.

Agencies established to help children enforce their rights are not sure-fire guarantees of high-quality service. There may be less costly ways to put these ideas into practice, and the risks of bureaucratic ineffectiveness are substantial. We can take a chance on less supervision just as we can take a chance on unpaid and uncertified agents. Here, too, there are ways to minimize the risks to some extent. For example, to the extent that the work of agents is open to public scrutiny and not done secretly, the question of supervision becomes less crucial. Agents will have peer pressure and widely known standards to live up to. We would not need to have supervisors "boss" agents in order to correct or critique their work. In resisting the bureaucracy of child agency, I am not arguing for private arrangements between children and their agents. In the end, it would be ineffective to make the availability and accountability of agents depend entirely on the good will of adults who could be convinced to take on the work or on the initiative of the self-motivated. It would be a little like having a right to medical care in a society that did not provide for the training of doctors or the building of hospitals but did nothing to prevent these things, either. If we acknowledge the injustice of the double standards of rights, then we should take steps as a society to bring it to an end. If we leave it to individuals to overcome as best they can, we undermine the seriousness of the problem.

I want to reemphasize that while I think the difficulties of institutionalizing child agents will be substantial, I have not argued that they cannot be overcome. It is not easy to deliver social services effectively, and our systems often get out of hand. Our experience with these matters tends to show that we do relatively better with small systems than with large ones in terms of getting them to do what we had in mind in the first place, and in terms of overcoming difficulties which crop up from time to time. That is another reason why it is better to proceed with children's rights when and where we can, rather than throwing ourselves into large-scale social architecture. The issues of policy implementation will become less touchy in the future as it becomes clear that some things work and others do not.

Before bringing this speculation about the problems of institutionalizing child agency to an end, we need to look at what is in some respects the touchiest issue of them all: What is the relationship of the child agent to the child's family? To this point in the discussion, I have rather consciously assumed that the child agent might not be a parent. That is not because parents should never be agents—in some cases, they might make the best ones. Rather it is because I did not want to obscure the fact that this proposal will sometimes mean that a non-related adult will become involved in what have traditionally been areas of family prerogative. A commitment to equal rights for children will require us to accept this—and that means facing up to it squarely.

CHAPTER VII

Living with Children and Their Rights

If child agents are going to be effective, they are going to have to become involved with children—and that will mean getting involved with children's families. How they would do this, and to what extent, is not entirely clear, but a fairly typical reaction to the proposal of child agents is that such a system would undermine the authority structure of the family. In particular, the concern is that equal rights for children would interfere with parental control over child-rearing, and would create an impossible atmosphere in the family by bringing an outsider into its private functionings. One could conjure up images of unruly children—young thugs—pushing their helpless parents around, giving orders, refusing cooperation, being abusive, making demands, and smirking while they stand on their rights—backed up by an agent who is totally unsympathetic to the parents' plight. This nightmare is only that—but it arises from a concern we need to pay attention to: how would parents continue to govern families in a society with child agents?

Child governance is the other side of child protection. Children are supposed to be in need of protection because they are unable to run their own lives. But this inability also means that they need someone to run their lives for them. That job falls to their parents, for the sort of government that people who talk this way usually mean is monarchy. Why democracy, a form of governance we are more familiar with, is not invoked here is a question we will take up in the next chapter. At any rate, the family monarchy might not function very well if children were represented by agents who insisted that they be given their rights. There seem to be two main problem areas: the limitations which rights set on parental control, and the impact of an outside force on the strength of parental authority. Let us look at the issue of control first.

Does parental control over children require that children be denied their rights? In order to answer this question, we need to look at two distinct situations. First, consider a case in which a parent controls a child through physical punishment and the threat of it. If the child will not do as the parent demands, the parent will strike or beat the child to enforce compliance. Although there is some question about it, we can suppose that this is reasonably effective and that the child substantially does what the parent asks. Compare this to another case in which the parent controls the child through a system of conditional rewards. That is, the parent has a number of rules which she or he wishes the child to follow. Obedience to these rules is rewarded with privileges of various kinds which the child desires—but to which he or she is not, strictly speaking, entitled. Upon disobedience, the privileges are suspended or revoked. Here, too, we shall suppose that the system is reasonably effective and that the child complies with parental demands.

The point I want to develop here is that equal rights for children precludes the first sort of control, but not the second. In other words, it limits but does not eliminate the control which establishes an authority structure in the family. Control of the first sort depends on the fact that the child has no right against assault with respect to her or his parents. Parents and others, such as school teachers acting in the place of parents, are granted the right to use corporal punishment on children as part of the latitude they have to raise them as they see fit. There are limits, of course; parents do not have the right to abuse their children. Still, if one adult struck another adult under the circumstances in which it was permissible to strike her or his own child, we would treat the incident as simple assault. Assault is a fairly serious crime, and we have a right not to be subjected to it. If children had the same rights adults do, they would be protected against assault by their parents.

That, in turn, would mean that parents could not control their children by striking them or threatening to strike them.

In the second case we imagined, the parent exercised control by making certain privileges conditional on obedience to family rules. This tactic is familiar to everyone. If children get out of line, they are denied dessert, sent to bed early, not allowed to go to the movies, not permitted the use of the parents' car, bowling ball, or whatever. Since the child presumably wants these amenities, she or he has an interest in following the rules. The control is accepted by the child on the basis of a calculation—whether explicit or not—but it is very definitely in the parents' hands. There is no question that the parents are in a position to make the rules and that the resources which constitute the rewards are theirs or under their control. The thing to notice here is that this system of control operates entirely within the realm of privilege. In our society there are no such rights as the right to dessert, to stay up until midnight, to see a film each week, or to use another's automobile or bowling ball. Since adults do not have these rights against one another, we have no reason to argue that children should, either.

I am not saying that any or every system of rules and privileges which parents set up is good, or fair, or even acceptable. It may well happen that the rules are petty or arbitrary. Revoking a privilege can be mean, pointless, callous, counterproductive, or unjust in various circumstances. But even though it might be wrong for parents to insist on certain rules or punish non-compliance in a particular way, it is not a violation of their children's rights to do so.

Ronald Dworkin has described the difference between having a right to do something and doing the right thing:

There is a clear difference between saying that someone has a right to do something . . . and saying that it is the "right" thing for him to do, or that he does no "wrong" in doing it. Someone may have the right to do something that is wrong for him to do, as might be the case with gambling. Conversely, something may be the right thing for him to do and yet he may have no right to do it, in the sense that it would not be wrong for someone to interfere with his trying.[1]

This distinction can be useful to us here. As in the gambling example, the parent may have the right to use her or his own resources as rewards and yet it might be the wrong thing to do in certain situations—as, for example, a parent's revoking major privileges for an inadvertent slip-up on a somewhat trivial rule. The other side of this is that where the child does not have a right to a specific form of treatment by a parent the parent may, nevertheless, treat the child wrongly. This sort of wrong is not as serious as a violation of the child's rights, but it can be a wrong anyway. So to say that children should have the same rights as adults is not to say anything so extreme as that adults should have no control over their children or even anything so reasonable as that adults may not treat their children wrongly. It is only to say that they may not control them in ways which they could not use on other adults without violating their rights.

Control through conditional rewards is, to be sure, more limited than control through the threat of force. The limitation stems from the fact that the subject of the control must think it is "worth it" to seek the rewards of the system. If the rules are more objectionable than the rewards are valuable, the rational thing to do is to ignore the rules and forego the privileges. While this might be impossible if the child were locked into the system, a right to an alternative home environment puts limits on how bad things can get. If the system of conditional rewards is too onerous, the child should be entitled to find another. In practice, if children could really get out from under oppressive situations, the most unreasonable systems of conditional reward would probably disappear. This represents a *de facto* limitation on the methods which parents may use, but it does not undermine their control—for the child's alternative is not "no control," but rather, a different method. And the threat of leaving home cannot be used very often against a severe parent before it becomes a bluff.

There are other rights which would also set limits on parental control if children had them. For example, if children had the right to privacy, they would be able to keep some kinds of information from their parents, and they would have places which would be safe from scrutiny by others—parents included. Insofar as activities or places really are private, they are thereby beyond the control of others. Children presently experience very little of this, and the fact that parents have almost unlimited snooping rights contributes enormously to their power to control. Another right which would limit parental control is the right to dispose of one's own money. Parents presently have the right to their children's income, and children may not do anything with their money which requires a legal contract except through their parents. Thus, any economic leverage children might conceivably have to use as a counter-balance to parental control is fairly effectively undermined. If children did have the same economic rights as adults, they would have resources with which to bargain over the limits of that control. But even though these rights would subvert some forms of parental control, there remains a myriad of ways in which children are dependent on their parents—and with dependency there will be control. Despite equal rights, parents will be able to exercise control over their children.

So far we have been considering ways of controlling children without much regard for the goals parents might have in exerting this control. Presumably they want to bring up their children to accept certain values and have some particular outlook on life. While there are no guarantees that any system of control would actually achieve this, we need to ask whether the exercise of certain rights by children would prohibit this sort of education or indoctrination. For if that happened, it would be fair to say that equal rights for children undermined an important aspect of parental control.

I suspect that people's worst fears in this respect are groundless. Consider, for example, the parental prerogative to bring up a child in the religion of the parents' choice. Adults have freedom of religion. Would equal rights for children mean that a parent could not indoctrinate a resisting child? The short answer to this question is "no." The right to freedom of religion is a right against Congress to pass no laws establishing or favoring one denomination or another. If children have this right against Congress, too, it will not touch the question of religious education in the home.

The longer route with this question begins from the fact

that adults have a right to hold and express their own convictions. Though we may try to persuade them to change their views—as missionaries do—we usually do not tie the religious indoctrination of adults to a system of rewards as we do the religious indoctrination of children. Is it possible that revoking privileges for inappropriate religious attitudes is a violation of the right to hold and express convictions?

A lot is going to depend here on how we describe the parental use of the privilege system. If it seems like what is going on is a form of brainwashing, then we are dealing with an assault on the right to hold and express convictions. If, on the other hand, we are speaking of friendly persuasion, mild admonition, and gentle encouragement, no such assault is plausible. We do not have a general right not to listen to others, although we are sometimes harangued in ways that could violate our right to privacy. All this really shows, I think, is that parents may on occasion abuse their authority by failing to respect their children's rights in the course of educating them. But parents *need* not do this in order to do their job— and that is enough to show that children's rights do not have to interfere with parental objectives and responsibilities. When we stop to think of the specific rights which adults have, we should realize that they do not nullify relations of authority and control—although they may limit them. If adults can manage in this way, we should not worry too much that children will be unable to.

What I have had to say so far has addressed the issue of the impact of children's rights themselves on the structure of authority in the family. We still need to face the fact that some agent—who may be neither a relative nor a close friend— could become involved in intrafamily matters. This outside interference, as much as the actual rights, could cause great concern by those who see children's rights as dangerous to our most basic social arrangement.

Any discussion of "interference" with the family needs to be kept in perspective. If American families were ever self-sufficient, they surely are not that now. Every family is dependent in countless ways on the services of others such as teachers, doctors, merchants, spiritual advisors, den mothers, and now sometimes therapists and counselors. While it is usually the job of the parents to acquire the money necessary to keep the family going, they do not literally provide for their children's needs. Kenneth Keniston has described the function of the parent in American society as similar to the function of a business executive:

Most important, parents today have a demanding new role choosing, meeting, talking with, and coordinating the experts, the technology, and the institutions that help bring up their children. The specific work involved is familiar to any parent: consultations with teachers, finding good health care, trying to monitor television watching, and so on. No longer able to do it all themselves, parents today are in some ways like the executives in a large firm—responsible for the smooth coordination of the many people and processes that must work together to produce the final product.[2]

In other words, "outsiders" have become an integral part of family life.

It is important not to lose sight of this conception of the family. Self-sufficiency is no longer even an appropriate ideal. The family needs to draw on resources from without—and these outsiders are not one and all "interfering." Many of them are invited to play a part in family life, and some of them make contributions which are both significant and appreciated. So the suggestion that another outsider might play a role in family affairs is not, on its face, a violation of some fundamental principle we live by. The concept of child agents should not be dismissed because it rubs the myth of the self-sufficient family the wrong way. We need to look deeper to find the sore points.

I suspect that one of the main sources of resistance to the idea of child agents is that parents would find it embarrassing to have other adults watch them do their parenting. And child agents would not only be watching; they would be looking critically to see if the parents were violating their children's rights. Embarrassment in this situation is a perfectly legitimate response. I imagine that most parents would find this sort of supervision demeaning. A majority of parents in our society have not been supervised in this way, and probably have no taste for the experience. However, those parents who have had to depend upon social service agencies of one form or another (welfare departments, adoption agencies) have had the sort of experience we are worried about here. Indeed, it is this kind of supervision—and not only the meager level of funding—which is the source of a major complaint that the welfare system demeans human dignity. There is scant room for self-respect when a person has to justify life-style and daily habits to another who does not share them, may not understand them, and is in a position to force a change in them. Perhaps child agents, too, would be in a position to undermine the dignity of parents. That is not a danger to take lightly.

There are at least two things to say about this problem for child agency. The first is that the danger is real enough, and certain precautions would have to be taken to see to it that child agents did not come to function as general parent supervisors. In order to do this, it would be important to insist that child agents deal only with the exercise of rights and stay out of other advocacy functions. An agent might not like certain parental practices—their method of control, for example. But as long as those practices violated no rights, they should not be the business of the child agent. It might well be that the parents themselves do not like the method, and need some kind of help or advice. But that help should not come from someone who is potentially in conflict with them over questions of rights or someone who may be in a position to help force them to abandon certain practices which violate their children's rights. The child agent represents a formidable force, and the use of that kind of force beyond its proper limits in order to coax conformity to the agent's own sense of what a family should be like is a source of great indignity. To guard against this, the agent should only intervene in order to help a child secure specific rights or on specific charges of violation of rights. One and the same person should never be child agent and social service representative to members of the same family.

Another way to minimize the potential danger to parental self-respect is to insist that child agents never act to secure a child's rights against that child's wishes or over that child's objections. By imposing this condition, we are dealing with a trade-off of social benefits. If we accept it, we must also accept the fact that some children who are having their rights violated will be unwilling or unable to speak up, though they might under prodding from an agent. Yet we can accept this fact if we think that it will reduce the possible abuses of child agency sufficiently to improve the desirability and effectiveness of the system. Since an attack on dignity is such a serious thing, it is worth bending a little to try to avoid it. And this brings us to the next point.

Our concern for dignity cannot be restricted to the dignity of the parents. Interference with family practices is not the only way in which family members are demeaned. It is most demeaning to have one's rights violated. Children who are in that position are in need of an agent to help them restore their dignity as much as their parents need to feel that they are not being pushed around by impersonal or unsympathetic representatives of the state. In situations where an agent is likely to be called in, we may end up balancing one person's sense of dignity against another's. There may well be losers in these kinds of situations, but we can not require that the children always lose. And that is what the suggestion that we do away with child agency because it undermines parental dignity amounts to.

I want to consider one other objection to the interference by child agents with family affairs. That is that the child agent will become another authority figure and as such, undermine the parent's ability to instruct and socialize the child. The presumption here is that the child will become confused and not know which adult to listen to, or that the child will play one adult against the other and so dilute the effectiveness of both.

This is a very tricky argument, and those who are attracted to it must make it cautiously. If it is insisted upon too strongly, it begins to look like an argument for the superiority of single-parent families. Yet few people would be willing to say that the absence of a second parent generally improves the authority structure of the family. If there is anything to this objection, it must be a good deal more subtle than this. However, there is not really any support for subtle concerns about multiple authority figures in children's lives. In the first place, it is simply not true that a parent or two are the only authorities children must deal with. All school-aged children and the younger ones who have attended day care centers or neighborhood play groups are quite used to non-parental authorities. There is no particular reason to believe that this is confusing to children. They do not seem to find the phenomenom "unnatural" or worry excessively about whom to obey. This is not to say that there are never conflicts among authorities, but only that children, like the rest of us, seem capable of following those conflicts through to their resolution (when they are resolved) or accommodating them (when they are not). There is no special problem here which would require us to abandon child agency. In fact, given the choice, I think most of us would prefer to bring our children up in a society which emphasized a dispersal of authority throughout the community rather than a concentration of authority in a single individual or ruling clique.

Throughout this discussion, I have concentrated on the potential conflicts between child agent and parent. These are real possibilities and should not be ignored, but it is important to remember that children will not always be in conflict with their parents on issues of rights. We should expect that parents will, for the most part, be supportive of their children's rights. Many of the rights we are speaking of are not rights against the family, but against the state or society at large. But beyond that, it is *just* that children should have equal rights, and parents who come to see that may be less inclined to stand in the way. We should be optimistic here without becoming complacent or slackening our determination to bring these rights into being. Child agents cannot be hostile to parents, but they must steadfastly serve children.

CHAPTER VIII

The Right to Political Participation

In this and the following chapters, I plan to discuss in greater detail a few of the rights which children should have. It is not my intention to give a comprehensive list of rights, and I shall deliberately avoid some of the more controversial rights, such as those relating to sexuality. My aim here is to show that equal rights for children is a policy which is not only grounded in the dictates of social justice, but also one which we would be better off adopting. To be sure, for some rights we honestly have no idea what the effect of extending them to children would be. Since my powers of prediction are no better than average, I am not willing to go too far out on a limb with those rights. Where it really seems impossible to say what the effect of extending some right or another to children would be, reasonable people will proceed with caution. This is not back-sliding. The possibility that as a society we would come to regret granting children certain rights cannot be used as a justification for not making the effort, because the social justice argument of Chapters IV and V applies whether the consequences of the extension are beneficial or not. At any rate, in some areas prediction does not seem to be an unredeemably idle pastime. We can make some half-educated guesses about how our social policies will turn out, and I would like to explore the following areas: political rights, rights in court, and the rights of privacy, confidentiality, and access to information.

Before I plunge into speculation about what it would mean

to extend full political rights to children in our society, I need to say a few things about why there is no bill of rights for children to cap-off this discussion, and why it is important to go beyond considerations of social justice and raise the question of the impact of these proposals on social life.

There are numerous bills of rights for children. I have quoted one by Richard Farson in the first chapter; others differ in detail but make rather similar demands. These lists of rights are quite useful for bringing people to see that something more than child protection is at stake, and for providing examples to discuss and dispute. In spite of these services, a bill of rights can leave the impression that there is some special set of rights especially for children. This seems to me to be a misimpression, and I want to avoid it. Our response to the question "which rights should children have?" should be "the rights which presently belong to adults" (to the extent that we have been able to eliminate relevant differences). If we need a list, it is not a special list for children, but the list of rights which adults now have.

In other words, the program for pursuing a policy of equal rights for children should not be agitation for a new or special set of rights. Rather it should be a program to eliminate the legal and customary barriers which support the double standard and to begin to establish a system of child agents who have specific obligations of performance toward children. In this way we will end up with a single standard of rights. Then we will not be caught in the position of having to tinker with the "bill" as the rights of adults change or grow with time. Gains in rights for adults would and should be gains for everyone. Our present task should be an attack on existing obstacles rather than on the creation of new rights.

A successful attack on the double standard will probably require more than an insistence that justice demands its abolition. As attractive as the social justice strategy is, people are quite naturally reluctant to acknowledge it without having some idea about how the new arrangements will affect their lives down the road a little. Granting new rights or extending old ones to new groups is serious business. Indeed, it is all the more serious, because once the rights are acknowledged, it is too late to deny their exercise on the grounds that their effects are socially undesirable. This makes it all the more important to show how the extension of rights to children will be of general social benefit (where this is, in fact, true). The idea that rights take precedence over the good of society is one which we have not yet touched on, but it is of some importance here.

This feature of rights is at the core of Ronald Dworkin's analysis of that concept:

A successful claim of right, in the strong sense I described, has this consequence. If someone has a right to something, then it is wrong for the government to deny it to him even though it would be in the general interest to do so.[1]

*   *   *

Of course a responsible government must be ready to justify anything it does, particularly when it limits the liberty of its citizens. But normally it is a sufficient justification, even for an act that limits liberty, that the act is calculated to increase what the philosophers call general utility—that it is calculated to produce more over-all benefit than harm. So, though the New York City government needs a justification for forbidding motorists to drive up Lexington Avenue, it is sufficient justification if the proper officials believe, on sound evidence, that the gain to the many will outweigh the inconvenience to the few. When individual citizens are said to have rights against the Government, however, like the right of free speech, that must mean that this sort of justification is not enough.[2]

It is not enough because rights which could be abolished when the society would be slightly better off as a result would be so weak that we could not rely on our rights in hard times. So once we agree that something is a right for someone, we may not go on to complain that we object to the way they exercise it. Rather, we may complain, but the complaint should be ignored.

Because rights have this feature, it is important that we do not create rights which we think might be socially destructive. Since we cannot take the general interest into account after the fact, we have all the more reason to think about it beforehand. Extending equal rights to children should be done for reasons of social justice, but social justice is not the only thing of value in our world. If the cure of an injustice is worse than the injustice itself, then we should probably live with the injustice until a less destructive cure can be found. In light of the possibilities suggested here, we cannot simply abolish the double standard. We must first ask whether, according to our best guess, extending equal rights to children will make us better or worse off in the long run.

There is no way to answer this question in general. We must examine specific rights and try to imagine what it would be like to extend them to children. If on the whole it seems that we would be no worse off than we are now, then we should do it. If we would be better off, we should do it with more enthusiasm. In any event, the discussion in the last three chapters may be taken as a model for beginning the process of evaluating equal rights for children as a viable social policy. The case for extending political rights for children is in some ways the easiest to make because the relevant considerations are fairly clear. For that reason, I shall begin there.

Children should have all of the rights which entitle citizens to participate in the political process. That is, they should have the right to vote in elections at all levels of government; the right to run for elective offices which do not have special constitutional age requirements over and above the age of majority; the right to initiate petitions, referenda, and recall elections; the right to organize into legitimate political parties or join already existing ones as full members; and the right of access to all lobbying channels now open to adults. These are the main ways in which adults may participate in the political process in America, but should we devise others, children should have the right to use them as well. When I say that children should have these rights, I mean that all children should have them. There should be no barrier to political participation which is established solely on the basis of age.

What would happen to our society if children had the rights of full political participation? Some people have imagined that children could be a powerful force for social change in this country if they had access to the political machinery. Some of the people who think this long for the time when it will happen; in their view, things could only get better if political decisions were influenced by the perceptions of (uncorrupted) youth. Others dread the possibility; they believe that the (unstable) young would only make a bigger mess of society by jeopardizing order and stability for short-sighted ideals. These hopes and fears seem quite unrealistic to me, and I do not think we have to give them much room in our thinking about a policy of political rights for children.

Control over the political machinery in a large representative democracy such as ours does not fall to the largest group with a common interest. It does not "fall" to anyone. Political power is developed and maintained with the organization of party machinery, money, and patronage. The work is demanding and sophisticated. Those who wish to have an impact on political matters must be prepared to take them on as a fulltime job and a long-term project. This sort of time and energy is required whether one chooses to work from within the existing system or from without. Those working from within must demonstrate loyalty to the party, be willing to take on day-to-day drudge work, serve current leaders, and generally be willing to engage in an extended apprenticeship prior to assuming real influence—for it is one thing to lobby for some legislation or win an elective office, but quite another to break into the network of political control.

Those who work outside the traditional political machinery usually focus on single issues or specific areas of change. I am thinking here of organized lobbying groups (like the Children's Defense Fund), specific protest movements (like the Civil Rights Movement, and Anti-War Movement), and short-term coalitions (like environmentalists working to ban non-returnable bottles). This sort of political work is also demanding, time-consuming, and sophisticated. Since the people who are engaged in it are usually pitted against career politicians, they must be willing to devote extended energy to their cause if they hope to move unresponsive machinery. The point of these observations is that having the *right* to participate in politics cannot seriously be equated with having *control* over the political system. The right of participation may be necessary for any individual or group that wants to make a political impact on the society, but it is hardly sufficient—as women and blacks know all too well. Taking control of a political system in the face of entrenched opposition is not child's play.

As a matter of fact, it is highly unlikely that children as a group would have the time, energy, interest, or sophistication to organize themselves into concerted action. Some children might, of course, take an interest in politics—they might even devote themselves to it. But that is not what it would mean for children to have political control, either. To be a serious and distinct political force, some children would have to create organizations (with the help of agents) which sufficiently large numbers of other children would be willing to recognize and endorse as expressing their interests. Anything short of this would probably mean that children's political participation would not have the impact of a force in a single direction. Instead, children would distribute themselves along the political spectrum and undermine any group effect they might have had. It is not very likely that extending political rights to children would mean that they would enter the system as a force to be reckoned with. So we may set aside these more grandiose speculations about the impact of children's political participation in our social life, and turn to some of the more plausible worries.

Even if the wholesale inclusion of children in the political process did not have a very substantial influence on our governmental policies, some people have speculated that it would make the process itself less effective or less efficient—or even, perhaps, impossible. In other words, our form of government would be weakened in important ways if children were permitted to participate in it. One of the most explicit proponents of this view is Carl Cohen, who takes up the question of the political participation of children in his book, *Democracy*.

Cohen argues that democracy requires a community of rational members in order to work successfully—or even to work at all.[3] Children, in his view, are marginal members and so "are normally and properly excluded from full participation in politics."[4] They are marginal because they do not have the capacity to participate—that is, they lack "reasonable maturity or rationality."[5] In another place he says:

The absence of such rationality is the reason it makes little sense to talk of democracy among brutes, or infants. It is not just that they cannot operate a democracy well; they cannot operate it at all.[6]

If children were really *unable* to participate in the political process, then it would be idle to insist that they be entitled to do so. It would make about as much sense as extending the right to the inhabitants of Mars. For different reasons, neither group could take us up on the offer. But Cohen has not shown that children are unable to participate, and he has certainly not shown that the participation of "marginal members" would weaken the system.

In the first place, not all children are infants—and most of them are emphatically not brutes. From what we know of children's sense of politics, they seem to develop rather rudimentary notions about government by the age of five, and understand it pretty well sometime after age ten or eleven. R. W. Connell, one of the more sensitive researchers on this topic, sums up the child's political development this way:

From the 5 year old's bower-bird collection of bits about important people, to the 15 year old's knowledge of an intricately organized political world, is an immense and impressive change. It is gradual; there is no sudden appearance at any one age of a picture of the political order. The construction work goes on right through childhood and adolescence, and no doubt into adulthood, as more information comes in; but there is a period, around the ages of 10 and 11, when the work goes on most rapidly and its results show most vividly. With a little dramatic license, we may speak of the last years of primary school as the period of the construction of the political order.[7]

Children manage to understand the political process much sooner than Cohen would have us believe; and they seem to do this without overly much indoctrination—and, of course, without the hope of participation. So although some children may be unable—incapable—of participation, this is not true of children generally.

In the second place, *operating* a democracy is not the only legitimate form of participation, as Cohen implies in the quotation above. It is surely true that infants could not operate a democracy; but why think that they would be called upon to do so? We are not talking about children establishing their own community with their own government, but about their participation in our political community along with adults. Democracy does not presuppose that *every* member can operate it, but only that some can. Indeed, in groups larger than fifty or sixty members, it would probably be ineffective or inefficient to try to have everyone run the show. And it would be impossible to require that sort of participation from everyone in a society of millions. So one can hardly say that it would weaken a democracy to have some members participating who could not operate the government. As long as there are enough people around who can operate it, the others might find different forms of participation which would not subvert the efficiency of the process. The real question here is not whether children are able to participate, but whether in doing so they would somehow undermine the workings of democracy.

The idea that the wholesale influx of children into the political system could gum up the works is suggested by Clyde Evans in "Children's Rights: The Incompetence Objection." He is not talking about the rights of political participation exclusively, but his remarks should be understood as applying to those rights as well. Evans is willing to presume that a substantial number of children are, in fact, incompetent to exercise certain rights. And he would deny rights to the incompetent because

Wholesale admission of them as full-fledged members of the society—i.e. as possessors of rights—could so "unbalance" the system as to wreak havoc. The infusion of such large numbers of incompetents might prove more than the system could handle.[8]

In other words, in the case we are discussing, children would be able to participate in the political process, but the quality of the participation would have a debilitating effect on the political system. If the unqualified extension of political rights to children would really wreak havoc, denying them participation might be the lesser evil. Is that plausible?

To answer this question let us try to imagine the ways in which children could have a harmful effect on the political process. To do this we will assume the worst, namely that their political behavior would be unrelentingly childish. (The reader may surmise that I do not accept this assumption, but it is time to muster all the doom and gloom we can.) I can think of three ways in which childishness *might* wreak some havoc: as thoughtlessness, as a taste for the bizarre, and as helplessness.

Suppose that children participated in politics throughlessly. The sort of thoughtlessness I have in mind here is the unthinking sort rather than the small-regard-for-the-feelings-of-others variety which is more common to adults. The political acts of thoughtless children would be casual rather than planned, erratic rather than systematic, occasional rather than regular, and perhaps more than a little arbitrary. Thoughtless action is also taken without due regard for its consequences. So we might expect that thoughtless children would not operate with much self-restraint when they acted in this way.

People whose participation had this character would certainly not be very constructive, but they can hardly be accused of doing much damage. Actions which are thoughtless in this way are usually ineffective as well. Now this kind of ineffectiveness would be harmful coming from political leaders, but why assume that thoughtless children could ever become leaders? As we have pointed out, political control requires diligence, a certain kind of skill, and the willingness to serve a substantal apprenticeship to the current leaders. These are exactly the things that the thoughtless person would be unable to do. It is highly implausible to suppose that children with this deficiency would ever be in the positions of leadership from whence the damage would be done. Thoughtless people who are not in positions of control—even large numbers of them—do not act in concert, so we should not worry that they could force an ill-advised policy on the rest of us through sheer strength of numbers. If they could, it would be a strong indication that they were not really thoughtless after all.

A second kind of "childish" behavior which causes some people to worry about equal political rights for children is the expression of bizarre preferences. "Bizarre" might be overstating the case to some extent, but the fear is that children might well, *en masse*, support Snoopy for president or Santa Claus for governor. To have to deal with such frivolity in the course of serious political decision-making would be at best distracting, and at worst paralyzing. There are more and less grave variations on this argument. In its hysterical form, it raises the spectre of the constitutional crisis which could follow the election of a make-believe character to one of the nation's highest offices. A more plausible concern is that campaigns for Snoopy or Santa Claus make a mockery of the political process and encourage people to discount the value of their political rights. A third worry in this vein is that children would prefer candidates for the "wrong" reasons, and that ultimately candidates would have to pander to these tastes in order to be elected. Should some candidate actually promise free movies and a bubble gum machine on every corner, *adults* would lose confidence in the political process.

What lies behind the various forms of this argument and makes children's preferences politically relevant is the belief that members of a political community must, at some level, trust the judgment of the other members. They must do this because otherwise they will not be able to abide by decisions made according to the principle of majority rule. In other words, if we cannot trust children's judgments because we think of children as having bizarre preferences, we will not be willing to rely on a political system which makes it possible for them to work their will.

Here, as with the worries about children's thoughtlessness, the realities of political power and control in our country suggest that these concerns are rather exaggerated. People who prefer Snoopy for president and free movies do not rise to positions of political importance, nor are they treated with much respect by those who have such importance. In adults, these preferences are treated as symptoms of a demented mind; in children they are taken as signs of frivolity or immaturity. And the frivolous and immature do not make very effective political organizers.

Beyond this, our political system does not really depend on the tightly-knit community of mutually respecting members which give point to the concern. We do not live in a small direct democracy, but a large representative one. Very few decisions are made by simply counting heads. Indeed, our political system was designed explicitly to take factionalism and irresolvable conflict of interest into account. There are plenty of groups in society which do not like one another's tastes or trust one another's judgments. This may make them careful or crafty, but it does not lead them to reject the political process (for the most part). How else could they hope to work their will? There is enough serious mutual distrust in all quarters of our society to make raising the issue of "community" against the inclusion of children in the political process seem rather hypocritical.

One final concern about the "childishness" of children in politics needs to be raised here. That is the worry that children are pretty much helpless, and would constitute a drain on the political system. The idea here is that in a political society everyone has to do her or his part. Those who constitute a passive presence only make more work for the others. And the result of overburdening the more active elements of the body politic is that they will end up doing their work less efficiently.

As usual, this sort of argument idealizes the quality of the typical adult's participation by singling out the likelihood of passivity from children and ignoring the realities of political power. But setting those observations aside, we should also notice that the governance of children is not an *additional* burden which society would take on when it made them full members. Children are governed now—as marginal members. The difference in status would only mean that those who presently have no chance of participating in their own governance would, with political rights, have the opportunity to take on a share of the task. This can hardly be supposed to make the work of political leaders more burdensome than it already is. At most one might make a case that the extension of political rights to children would place an additional burden on child agents. This may well be true, but it is not particularly devastating—for we have no particular reason to anticipate a serious shortage of child agents.

I do not want to say that it is inconceivable that the granting of political rights to children will weaken the existing political system, but I do not think this is very likely. Those who raise this problem have not been able or willing to paint a very convincing portrait of how things would break down. I have tried to suggest some of the most plausible ways that this might happen, and show why I do not find them very convincing. Of course, a person should always be willing to revise her or his opinions in the face of new evidence, so I would not claim to have spoken the last word on this subject.

The news that children as a group would probably not have an overwhelming impact on the political system if given the right to participate will come with sorrow to some and relief to others. In any event, the question we are left with is "what impact will the political system have on children who are able to participate in it?" Here again we shall try to fathom whether society would be better or worse off for the experience.

Large numbers of children—certainly most of those under the age of five—may have no interest whatsoever in the political system. If they do not, then they will simply ignore it and live much as they do now. It is worth remembering that having the right to participate is not the same as being required to participate. Having a right to something gives a person the *option* of doing it or having it. The right to participate will just not mean anything to the child who is unable to or uninterested in pursuing it. Nothing is gained, but nothing is lost, either, by extending the vote to them.

Some people worry that children who have political rights without the concomitant interest will be exploited by their parents. The parents, it is said, will coax their children into voting in accordance with the parents' own preferences. Thus, an unscrupulous parent will use an unsuspecting child in order to acquire additional political strength. This would be unfair to the rest of society, and damaging to the parent-child relationship.

The first thing to say about this is that in most elections there is not much incentive to have an additional vote or two. In an election with fifteen or twenty thousand voters, one vote more or less does not add up to much clout. Even if the practice were widespread, it would have to be one-sided as well if it were to make any difference in the outcome. But the more relevant point to make here is that the idea of child agents is designed to deal with just this sort of worry. If children do not have the capacities necessary to resist exploitation of their rights, then someone without a conflict of interest must be obligated to help the child exercise those rights. In this case we might require that an agent other than the child's parent be assigned to the child at the time she or he registers to vote. The agent could have, among other duties, the job of attesting that the child was not being used simply as a parental tool. This might add a little time to the registration process, but it would adequately meet the anticipated difficulty.

The more interesting impact of the right to political participation for children will be on those who choose to exercise these rights. Some children will take them quite seriously and get involved in politics with an intensity and absorption which is occasionally seen in stamp collecting or in sports. It is hard to imagine anything very bad coming of this. Political defeats are sometimes bitter—but they are rarely fatal. There is usually a new battle, a new issue, a new candidate to throw one's energies into. And, if anything, the defeats are less immediate and less stinging than those children experience more regularly in organized sports or in competition in school. So it would not make much sense to deny children these rights in order to shield them from the sting of defeat. That much protection never has been a social priority for us.

The case for extending political rights to children can, in fact, be made more positively than I have so far. Participation in politics is not only a fair method of making decisions; it is a means of developing the capacities and abilities of citizens. This has been a traditional aim of and justification for an extensively democratic form of government. As Carole Pateman put it:

The major function of participation in the theory of participatory democracy is . . . an educative one, educative in the widest sense, including both the psychological aspect and the gaining of practice in democratic skills and procedures. . . . [T]he more individuals participate the better able they become to do so."[9]

Many of the theorists who accepted this aim of a democratic form of government were nevertheless unwilling to admit children into the process. J. S. Mill is the prime example. But there is no very good reason to suppose that people would be better off waiting eighteen or twenty-one years to begin this sort of education. Indeed, G. B. Shaw has suggested a very good reason why we should not:

A nation that is free at twenty-one is not free at all; just as a man first enriched at fifty remains poor all his life, even if he does not curtail it by drinking himself to death in the first wild ecstacy of being able to swallow as much as he likes for the first time.[10]

If we are interested in more extensive political participation than we now have in our society, then it can only be to our benefit to involve people early. To do so would be to give politics for some a seriousness which it now lacks. I do not mean that those who presently participate do not do so seriously. But owing to the age barrier, all who come to politics come to it late. For an eighteen or twenty-one year old, political participation has the status of a career choice rather than a social activity. If politics should be something that we do in addition to our work, we should begin doing it early— before the competition for our interest becomes too heavy.

As far as I can see, equal rights to political participation for children will not weaken or fundamentally change our governmental system. At best it will pave the way for a goal of democratic theory which has largely been ignored in recent times (the educational function of participation). At worst, things will go on largely as they do now. In either event—or any in between—there is no compelling reason to continue the injustice of denying political participation to children.

CHAPTER IX

Rights in Court

One area in which children are generally thought to be better off for having a special standard of treatment is in their contact with the court system. The juvenile court system is regarded, on the whole, as a better "deal" for youthful offenders than they could expect to have in adult criminal courts. Indeed, in some ways the juvenile court system, in theory, represents the ultimate expression of the caretaker ideology: the child has a right "not to unrestrained liberty, but to custody."[1] The court, acting as a parent, will take firm but benevolent control of the child and guide her or him to a socially acceptable course of life. The aim, in contrast to the adult court system, is utterly non-punitive. Seen in this light, the double standard appears to work to the advantage of children.

Despite the good intentions of its originators, the juvenile court system bars children from exercising important rights in their dealings with the law: namely, the rights having to do with due process of law as they are spelled out in the Constitution. An end to the juvenile court system as it is presently conceived would bring these rights to children. I am not recommending this merely to be consistent in my opposition to a double standard. It seems to me that the return to a single standard of criminal justice would be in the best interests of children and of society as well. I say this with the full realization that the adult criminal justice system offers little opportunity for most who come before it to take full advantage of their rights in a meaningful way.

Equal rights for children in our courts would include rights which have nothing to do with what we normally think of as the criminal law. Children would have the right to initiate civil suits (it is presently a privilege granted them in some states under the auspices of an adult appointed to take the legal action for them). They would also have the right to representation in divorce and custody cases (again, this is presently possible, but not as a right). These rights are important, and they would have interesting social ramifications. Imagine, for example, divorce as a suit involving all the members of a family, and not merely the spouses. But as complicated as it might be to grant children these kinds of rights, the really serious reservations about the abolition of the double standard before the law have to do with these areas in which juvenile courts have jurisdiction— dependency and delinquency.

The category of dependent child goes back to the first juvenile court law in this country (Illinois, 1899). A dependent or neglected child was one who

. . . for any reason is destitute or homeless or abandoned . . . or who habitually begs or receives alms, or who is found living in any house of ill-fame or with any vicious or disreputable person, or whose home, by reason of neglect, cruelty, or depravity on the part of the parents, guardian, or other person in whose care it may be, is an unfit place for such child.[2]

There are two lines of concern which run through this definition. One has to do with the child's care and safety; the other with the child's moral environment. These are not very well distinguished, and I suppose that in the minds of the early twentieth century reformers they pretty much came to the same thing. But the difference is worth noticing, for I do not wish to contest the idea that a court may impose an obligation on someone to tend to the care and safety of a person who needs it— where such tending is required and requested. I expect that we would have our courts look after the very old, the retarded and the disabled in this way, and it may also be appropriate for some children in certain situations. However, this sort of dependency is not peculiar to children, and we would not need special juvenile courts to deal with it.

The other line of concern has to do with the child's moral environment, and is motivated by a desire to save children from their lower class lives. Where a child is not otherwise being abused or neglected, this is a hopeless job for the courts. In the first place, judges have been traditionally insensitive to the difference between an environment which was actually morally dangerous to the child and one which was simply different from the judge's own. In the second place, the courts do not have places to put the children they save. Foster homes can not accommodate them all, and "homes," "training schools," jails and other institutions of confinement are at least as morally dangerous as the most disreputable of families. But finally, the very idea that the lower class way of life can be eliminated for the next generation by the wholesale transfer of its children into the middle classes is mad. It is simply oblivious to a social and economic structure which cannot function without the working poor and the unemployed. This sort of child-saving is not the proper business of the courts. It is possible that the reformers of the late nineteenth century did not understand this, but the same ignorance is inexcusable in a judge sitting in the 1970's.

So we are left with delinquency as the serious business for the juvenile court system. Children below a specified age (typically sixteen years) are not subject to criminal prosecution. Instead, they may be adjudged delinquent and placed under the supervision of the court until they reach the age of majority (or sooner at the court's discretion). A delinquent was originally "any child under the age of 16 who violates any law of this State or any City or Village ordinance" (Illinois, 1899). But this definition was regarded as too narrow; by 1970, it was expanded as follows:

The words "delinquent child" shall mean any male child who while under the age of seventeen years or any female child who while under the age of eighteen years, violates any law of the State; or is incorrigible, or knowingly associates with thieves, vicious or immoral persons; or without just cause and without (the) consent of its parents, guardian or custodian absents itself from its home or place of abode, or is growing up in idleness or crime,

or knowingly frequents a house of ill-repute; or knowingly frequents any policy shop or place where any gaming device is operated; or frequents any saloon or dram room or bucket shop; or
wanders the streets in the night time without being on (any) lawful business or lawful occupation; or habitually wanders about
any railroad yard or tracks or jumps or attempts to jump on any
car or engine without lawful authority; or uses vile, obscene, vulgar,
profane or indecent language in (any) public place or about any
school house; or is guilty of indecent or lascivious conduct; any
child committing any of these acts herein shall be deemed a delinquent child.[3]

Most states define delinquency similarly today; indeed, the
major difference is that truancy from school has been added
to the list.

The question of whether children are better or worse off
under this double standard in court is a complicated one—in
part because we are dealing with four standards, not two. There
is, first, the juvenile court system in theory. Here the standard
of treatment specifies that no child under a certain age is a
criminal, that the job of the court is to help form young characters, and that the judge does this as a parent, in the child's
best interest, with individualized attention, in a private and
non-adversarial proceeding.

Secondly, there is the actual juvenile court system which is a
legal bureaucracy much like the adult criminal courts. It appre-
hends children rather than arresting them. After an intake interview, the court may file a delinquency petition charging acts of
delinquency which need not be specified, or may be changed
during the hearing. The court then holds a hearing which is
governed by minimal procedural standards (since the Gault
decision) to determine the best interests of the child and the
community. A case is disposed of by dismissal, suspension of
finding, probation, or commitment to an institution or foster
home.[4] Since juvenile courts are local institutions, the actual
systems vary considerably from place to place. This description
is, of necessity, rather crude. The discrepancy between the reality and the theory of the juvenile court system has been extensively studied, and is admitted by most thoughtful observers.
Our discussion must take account of the fact that there are two
standards of juvenile justice.

Likewise, there are two standards of justice in the adult criminal courts. The court system, in theory, operates according to the constraints set down in the Constitution and the Bill of Rights. (Almost all of these now apply to state as well as federal courts.) The general requirement is that a person may not be deprived of life, liberty or property without due process of law. More specifically, a person brought before a court has a right to indictment by a grand jury, a right to counsel, to a speedy and public trial, a statement of charges, and an impartial jury. During the proceeding, one also has the right to suppress evidence not properly obtained, a right to confront witnesses, to call one's own witnesses, and to avoid incriminating oneself. Furthermore, one has a right not to be placed in jeopardy twice for the same crime, and not to be sentenced in a cruel and unusual manner. Many of these rights have been elaborated in greater particularity in subsequent court decisions. As a body they constitute the standards of criminal procedure—in theory.

In reality, most trials bear little resemblance to the process these rights describe. This is not because these rights are normally flaunted or rejected by judges, but rather because the overwhelming number of defendants never actually go to trial. The actual criminal justice system is built on plea-bargaining: the practice of extracting an agreement from the defendant to plead guilty in exchange for a lesser charge or a lighter sentence. Since guilty pleas do not require trials, many of the rights of criminal procedure are irrelevant. (One still has several rights, including the right to a grand jury indictment, to counsel, and to protection against cruel and unusual punishment.) Since the plea-bargaining system is informal and gives great discretion to prosecutors and judges, it tends to discriminate against the poor who cannot hire competent lawyers, and must settle for lawyers appointed by the court who are usually too overworked to do an adequate job.

By now the reader should be able to sense the complication involved in evaluating the juvenile court system. Should we say that the juvenile system in actuality is worse than the ideal of the criminal justice system? Or should we compare it to the actual criminal justice system? Perhaps it is unfair to use the reality of the juvenile justice system as a standard at all, for it might be possible to do away with the worst practices—as the U.S. Supreme Court has started to do. If we are willing to grant that possibility, perhaps we should compare the standards of juvenile justice in theory to the standards of criminal justice in theory. Or would it be less naive to compare them to the actual practices of the criminal justice system?

Since an end to the juvenile justice system is not an easy thing to demand, it is important that in our evaluation we give it every benefit of the doubt. Thus, although the informality of the procedure is widely abused to the detriment of children, we shall assume that these abuses might be corrected. And in spite of the fact that every adult has a right to a trial by jury in serious criminal cases, we shall assume that it is not likely that many juveniles would have such trials if their cases were brought before a criminal court. In other words, the most difficult comparison is between the juvenile justice system in theory and the criminal justice system in reality. Still, even if we accept this as the double standard for children and adults, I would suggest that society (including children) would be better off if we did away with it, for the very idea of juvenile justice embodies the worst elements of the caretaker ideology.

The original underlying principle of the juvenile justice system is that "no child . . . shall be considered or be treated as a criminal; that a child under that age shall not be arrested, indicted, convicted, imprisoned, or punished as a criminal" (Tuthill). It is important to understand this principle in the right light; this is not a version of "boys will be boys." The intent is not to down-play the significance of delinquency, or to see youthful deviance as a normal part of growing up, or to keep children away from contact with the court. The idea, rather, is that children should not be "branded" as criminals or thrown into the same institutions with adult criminals (lest the disease be contagious). In other words, children should not be subjected to the legal process *as criminals*; but they may very well be subject to it *as delinquents*. The process need not be very different as long as it is called something else and sends the offenders to their own institutions. There is in this principle no renunciation of control over the young by the state.

Control is, in fact, a main element of the juvenile justice

theory. The juvenile court is on a moral mission: child saving. In order to save children, the court must take them in hand and exercise some control over their lives. The early champions of the juvenile court movement were quite explicit on this point. One of the more famous juvenile judges, Ben Lindsay, put it this way:

These children do not know how to obey. We want to teach them how and why. They must learn to respect the law, to respect authority, to respect the rights of others, for their own good and happiness as well as that of others. This is the first step in reform. If the home in which this duty rests can not do it, the state must; and in performing this function, a purely parental one, it must frequently deal with the home, the parent, and the child. The state must handle the problem as a wise parent would. It never has and never can do this through jails, prisons, and criminal courts as such.[5]

This passage contains many of the elements of the juvenile justice philosophy—the state as parent, the rejection of punishment (as such), a benevolent attitude toward children—but what is most striking about it is the concern Lindsay shows for the development of the child's character. Observance of the law is not enough; the judge wants respect as well. This is a heavy dose of intrusion from a state which professes to stay out of the private lives of its citizenry, but the enticement of saving the children helped to set that principle aside. Lindsay ends the paragraph from which the previous quotation is drawn with missionary zeal, singing the praises of the juvenile court as the instrument of salvation: "But I predict that we are on the eve of a great awakening, when the dark blot [treating children as criminals] will be obliterated in the refulgence and radiance of new methods [the juvenile court] founded in the love and teaching of our Divine Master and the tenderness of a mother for an erring child."[6] Such noble sentiment is hardly designed to make one very circumspect about the limits of control which judges may exercise over children. Quite the contrary. When salvation is at stake, the more the better.

The sort of control which the juvenile courts exercise is not the traditional control of the state over its citizenry. It is the control of a parent. The doctrine which transforms the judge into a father is called *parens patriae*. The phrase means that the state is the "common guardian of the community." What *that* means is not entirely clear—but when applied to children it has come to mean that the education and development of the child is of such importance to the state, that the right of control over the child ultimately rests with the state (although in most cases it is left to the parents). Armed with this doctrine, which had been made explicit in *ex parte Crouse*, judges came to think that they could literally be fathers to the poor and misguided youth who entered their chambers. For they were not standing in for the parent—it was the parents who had been standing in for them (and not doing a very good job of it at that). The sort of fatherhood which judges seemed to prefer, at least in their writings on this subject, was the awe-inspiring variety: a stern exterior with a core of benevolence which the contrite offender might tap. This is old-fashioned fatherhood, not modern parent-hood, and even women judges were expected to exhibit these traits. This style was adopted partly to provide a respectable role model for the morally disadvantaged child, but most judges also remark that it is a good technique for obtaining confessions. But whatever the motive, the effect was to transform a legal doctrine designed to justify state intervention in private life into an attempt to use the juvenile court to establish a *personal* relationship between judge and child.

The judge, as father, aims to act in the best interest of the child. What this means for the juvenile court philosophy is that the system, strictly speaking, does not punish children. I say "strictly speaking" because the point being made here is some-what technical. On the juvenile justice theory, the child should not be punished in the retributive sense of "an eye for an eye." That is, juvenile courts are not in the business of returning harm for harm. Whatever they might do to the child—it is for her or his own good. The juvenile court philosophy also rejects pun-ishment as general deterrence. That is, judges should not use the child to set an example for others. Even if harsh treatment of shoplifters would prevent *other* children from stealing mer-chandise, juvenile judges should not regard that as a good rea-son to hand out such sentences. This does not mean that they should not hand out harsh sentences, but only that they should do so when it is in the best interest of the child. Punishment, it seems, is to be defined by the intent of the giver rather than by the effects on the receiver. What the juvenile justice philosophy intends is that the child's experience in court be formative. A formative experience is one that helps to mold the child's character or set the direction of the child's life. Children, unlike adults, are not yet fixed in their ways—so the theory goes. A little judicial control at the right moment is designed to "fix" the child for good instead of evil. If this means restraining the child's liberty through probation or even incarceration—so be it. The judge is, at least, not punishing the child.

Instead of liberty, the child is entitled to custody. Custody is the form of supervision which is theoretically tailored to the child's needs. Ideally, the judge will determine how much supervision the particular child before her or him requires, and prescribe that amount. There are no fixed sentences for kinds of offenses—no "going rate" for larceny, rowdiness, incorrigibility, joy riding, and so on. The judge sentences the offender instead. One child may stop stealing and respect the law because of a good stern lecture or an appearance in court; another may have to spend his entire adolescence in a training school to achieve the same result. Mostly, however, the juvenile courts rely on probation (in approximately half the cases disposed of) to provide the kind of supervision which each child is said to need in variable degrees.

The main structural feature which distinguishes juvenile from criminal courts is that juvenile courts are supposed to be non-adversarial. In other words, there are not two sides—prosecution and defense—trying to, respectively, prove and disprove a charge in accordance with strict rules of combat. Juvenile courts have traditionally discouraged representation of the child by counsel, and have viewed insistence on fixed procedures as obstructionist. In theory this disdain for procedure indicates a desire for flexibility and informality rather than laxity.

The difference in procedure between juvenile and criminal courts is for many judges an essential one for maintaining the distinctiveness of the juvenile justice philosophy. This distinctiveness has been obscured considerably by the Supreme Court's 1961 decision *In re Gault*. There, for the first time, standards of courtroom procedure were required for juvenile trials. The procedures were explicitly adversarial: 1) Notice of the charges. 2) Right to counsel. 3) Right to confrontation and cross-examination. 4) Privilege against self-incrimination.[7] While setting these standards, the Supreme Court denied that it was obliterating the difference between juvenile and adult courts. This may have been wishful thinking on their part, or it may have been a signal that they would accept a rather narrow interpretation of the *Gault* decision. At any rate, various organizations of juvenile court judges expressed some displeasure with the decision; and there is evidence that it has not had a very substantial impact on the outcome of cases that go to juvenile court.[8] The point is that *Gault* goes against the grain of juvenile justice theory, and those who embrace the theory tend to see it as an obstacle more than an aid.

There is finally the matter of privacy. As a family affair, the juvenile court proceeding is supposed to be shielded from public view as much as is possible and practical. This is partly to avoid branding the child—a concession that "delinquent" is not a stigma-free label. But it is also intended to create the right sort of atmosphere for a benevolent proceeding and to prevent public humiliation from interfering with the rehabilitative process.

These, then, are the main elements of the juvenile justice philosophy. They constitute the best that the double standard has to offer. For our concern here is not so much with the ways in which the juvenile courts fail to live up to these ideals, but rather with the adequacy of the ideals themselves. It is no secret that not all judges are benevolent, fatherly, non-punitive, or concerned about individualized treatment of the children who come before them. And the fact that some children's lives are in the hands of hostile and powerful judges is a serious defect in the system. But it is not the defect I want to pursue here. As I see it, even at its best, this system deals with children without respecting them, and so offers them very little in the way of support or of help. This will be clear if we look at each of the elements a little more critically. Beyond that, there is a more basic flaw in this gem—a court of law is the wrong sort of institution for shaping young characters.

The first thing to notice about the definition of delinquency is that it is extremely broad and, at crucial points, extremely vague. The court may find a child delinquent for the company he or she keeps or for not showing sufficient deference to parental commands. There are no strict tests for "incorrigibility," "idleness," or "associating with immoral persons." The rationale for this is that the court needs the power to reach children who are in strict compliance with the letter of the adult criminal law, but who are "headed for trouble" or who do not sufficiently respect authority. The price we pay for granting juvenile judges this power is that there is not a child in America who is not technically a delinquent if someone wishes to press the case. Delinquency is as much a matter of how others interpret a child's actions as it is a matter of what those actions are. If a parent or teacher says that a child has a bad attitude, how is the child to acquit her or himself? In fact, there is no defense against delinquency beyond an appeal to the benevolence of the judge. The scope of the definition of delinquency makes a hearing on the merits of the issue quite dangerous for the child. There is always the risk that a strong argument for innocence may be taken as a sign of unwillingness to cooperate with the court. That is another ground for a finding of delinquency in some quarters. This sort of power seriously undermines the possibility of respect by the court for the child. The child cannot ask for respect; it is too dangerous. And the court cannot give it; it is so powerful that its gestures could not be taken seriously.

The second tenet of the juvenile justice philosophy—child-saving—is also not entirely without its problems. Setting aside the question of whether any of the means the court has for this task (probation, incarceration, etc.) are suitable to it, we might well wonder whether children are being rescued in spite of themselves. Were children seeking out the courts, were they for the most part thankful for judicial interference in their lives, the moral mission of the courts might have some social value. But the parallel to the religious missions does not extend this far. Children are being told, not asked, to step forward and repent. The impulse to salvation is neither voluntary nor motivated by the internal convictions of the "sinner." In heaven, enforced salvation is not salvation at all; and it is hard to see how it could be on earth, either. The child may be wrenched from a bad environment, but to be "saved" from it requires a process of conversion which courts do not even attempt to undertake. So, even if child-saving were more than another name for the attempt to impose middle class mores and life-style on the poor, it would not add up to a genuine conversion process, occurring as it does in an alien and hostile context.

A deeper trouble with child-saving is that it is sometimes not really undertaken in the child's behalf at all. This is not much discussed anymore, but child-saving began as part of a more general reforming movement bent on the eradication of crime. As T. D. Harley, an early juvenile court enthusiast, put it: "If the crime disease should ever be destroyed the work of fumiga-tion must begin in the homes and with the children." It is as hard to be against good health as it is to be against salvation, but one should not overlook the fact that children are being used here—used as means to solve problems which are not of their making and not their reponsibility. Harley is not talking about present crime; he is talking about future crime. And if children are being saved from what they might do rather than what they have done, then it is not so obviously a favor to them. This puts the loftiness of the motives of child-savers in serious doubt.

A third tenet of the philosophy—that the state has the au-thority of a parent over its children (*parens patriae*)—is also more sentimental than it is good for children. This becomes clear if we take the image seriously and literally for a moment. Imagine a father, who has never seen his child, returning to the family at a time of crisis. Perhaps the child is in trouble or there is a serious conflict in the family. At any rate, father decides to settle the matter. He does not actually come home, for he is very busy with other people's problems as well. The rest of the family must see him where he works; indeed, they are summoned to him. Father takes charge authoritatively. Rely-ing primarily on second-hand information and not providing sufficient time for everyone to tell their stories, he makes his judgment and then dismisses everyone, leaving the details of his solution to be carried out by his employees. If this imaginary person seems like a terrible father, it is the *best* a judge could hope for in terms of a parental relationship to a child standing before him. There is no history of support, no personal rapport, no mutual trust, no expectation of continuing commitment. The judge is a stranger, and no legal doctrine can confer parental status on one who will not accept parental functions. It would be more honest and certainly less confusing to stop calling the judge's authority parental.

A fourth claim, that the state does not punish delinquents, is largely a linguistic fiction. The state does not call what it does to them punishment, just as parents may come to believe that they do not punish their children when they say "this is for your own good" before striking them. To decide whether something is punishment, we need to look at the facts as well as the words. In the adult world of criminal courts, there is no doubt that jail is punishment. Do we have jails for children? They may not be called jails, but as Lois G. Forer so clearly illustrates, the difference between a jail and a "youth home" is the difference between a legal word and a juvenile court word:

JAIL
A place in which a prisoner is confined, which he cannot leave without a court order. It has bars, walls, locks, and often a "hole," that is, a dark place of solitary confinement. A jail is manned by guards with guns and sticks.

CHILDREN'S VILLAGE, YOUTH HOME, DEVELOPMENT CENTER, JUNIOR REPUBLIC, ETC., ETC.
A place in which a juvenile is confined, which he cannot leave without a court order. It has bars, walls, locks, and often a "hole," that is, a place of solitary confinement. A Children's Village or other place of commitment is manned by counselors and cottage fathers and mothers who are often equipped with guns and sticks.[9]

Where the key differences are the age of the inmates and the titles of the guards, there is no case for saying that the youth institutions do not punish. They are structurally and functionally similar to places designed to punish. The juvenile courts will continue to punish children as long as they rely on involuntary incarceration or involuntary supervision—no matter how good their intentions might be.

Individualized treatment and the privacy of the proceeding are both ideas which are quite acceptable in theory. Both present problems when it comes to putting them into practice effectively, but it is not my intention to elaborate on these criticisms of the juvenile court system. It is enough to say that the court does not really have sufficient personnel or sufficient resources to determine what each individual child actually needs and then to provide it. The practical problems about privacy are slightly different; the very mechanism which keeps the child from the public eye keeps abuses in the process hidden as well.

We turn finally to the feature of the juvenile justice theory which has received the most attention in the last decade—the absence of strict procedure. The flexibility and informality of the juvenile court hearing was typically counted among the system's virtues until the publicity over *In re Gault* exposed a darker side of this issue. Gerald Gault, aged fifteen, was adjudged delinquent for making an obscene phone call. The maximum penalty for an adult committing that crime under the Arizona criminal code is $5 to $50, or imprisonment for not more than two months. Gerald faced up to six years in the Children's Detention Home. This disparity of punishment actually has nothing to do with procedure, but it was shocking enough to draw attention to the fact that Gerald's parents received no notification of the charges, were not advised to obtain· counsel, were not allowed to confront the complainant at the hearing, had no right to a transcript of the hearing, and no right to appellate review. Furthermore, Gerald was made to incriminate himself by the judge. Actually, Gerald only admitted to dialing the number, and the case against him was so weak that only a hearing which was this loose could have resulted in the conviction (that is, the finding of delinquency). The U.S. Supreme Court found the Arizona juvenile hearing procedure to be in violation of the Fourteenth Amendment "due process" clause on the four counts mentioned previously, but it explicitly denied that juvenile courts must abide by adult procedures generally.[10]

There are still plenty of problems with juvenile court procedures. Heresay evidence is not barred. Indeed, rules of evidence need not be followed in general. The charge of delinquency does not have to be specified in terms of specific acts. That means that a child brought into court for one reason may be found delinquent for an entirely different one, should it come to the judge's attention. Transcripts and appeals are still difficult to come by. Now, procedural rights were created explicitly to protect adults from the power of the state, so to the extent that they are withheld from children, we are denying children these protections. How is it that anyone could come to think that children are best served in this way?

The key to understanding this rather curious position is that the juvenile court is said to be non-adversarial. In other words, a hearing is not a contest, but an inquiry into the facts. There are two reasons why this is difficult to swallow. In the first place, the judge is not often a disinterested neutral party. When the state makes the complaint, the judge, as its representative, becomes an adversary. In the second place, the court maintains the right to deprive the child of liberty. Children know this (or their agents do) and so are in a contest with *someone* for their freedom—whether the court chooses to acknowledge it or not. But beyond this, even an inquiry into the facts requires some procedure if facts are to be separated from fiction. In the rush to reject adversarial procedures, juvenile courts have not stopped to look for others better suited to their aims. Instead, they have settled for none at all; and in the face of victims like Gerald Gault, talk of informality and flexibility has a hollow ring. Beneath all of these problems there is a fundamental flaw in the juvenile justice philosophy. In our official dealings with juveniles, we are torn between extending a helping hand or an iron fist. Children, we say, should not be punished; they should be controlled. But the institution which we choose to do the controlling is the court system—the institution most closely identified with punishment. The damage a person risks in going to court is just too great to allow the courts to function as helping institutions in our society. It is not enough to say that a child before the court will not be called a criminal, will not be punished, will be treated as one of the family, and so on. These things have to be true as well. And as long as the courts can bring the power of the state to force children into involuntary submission, these things will not be true. A helping hand should be less awesome in order to be more effective.

Despite the inherent flaws in the juvenile justice philosophy, there are no doubt some who have grave reservations about scrapping it when the alternative is the adult criminal court system. Why should we think that children would be any better off in those hallowed halls? After all, adults do not fare very well there, criminal courts are no less powerful than juvenile courts, and they are surely no more benevolent. What possible advantage could there be in sending children to them?

In point of fact, there are several advantages, not the least of which would be the abolition of the most vague definitions of delinquency. As we noted, a child may be charged with delinquency for attitudes as well as for acts, or for being idle, unruly, or incorrigible. The mere association with immoral types can bring a child before a juvenile court. These things are not crimes for adults, and they cannot be. The parallel laws, such as the law against being a suspicious person, have been found to be unconstitutionally vague. An end to the juvenile court system would mean an end to the status of delinquent, and with it an end to court control of unruly (as opposed to illegal) behavior. This does not mean that we would have to live with a more unruly youth, but only that we would have to deal with those problems outside the court system. The seriously disturbed can always be committed to institutions, just as seriously disturbed adults can. But those who are rebellious or insufficiently respectful of adults do not belong in courts, and the virtue of adult criminal courts is that there is no room for such children there.

Juveniles would also have greater procedural protection in criminal court than they do presently. Incredible as it seems, this would be so even under the plea-bargaining system as it is presently practiced. In one sense, *Gault* has evened things up for juveniles by requiring notification of charges and the right to have a lawyer before the hearing. For once an adult enters a guilty plea, the rights having to do with the admissibility of evidence, the confrontation of witnesses, self-incrimination, and appeal are not, strictly speaking, relevant. These rights can only be claimed during a trial, and with a plea of guilty, no trial takes place. But even though children who plea-bargained would not actually be able to claim these rights either, the existence of these rights works as a check on the plea-bargaining system. A plea-bargain is a "deal" and what the defendant has to deal with is the right to go to trial if the consequences of a guilty plea seem too severe. A prosecutor with a weak or ambiguous case, or a judge who does not want to fill the court calendar with too many trials, will have to listen to the defendant's demands up to a point. Apart from the threat of more severe treatment if the defendant makes the state go to the expense of having a trial, there is no way absolutely to prevent someone from exercising these rights. That is not so in juvenile court. Since the Supreme Court did not require transcripts or appeals for juvenile hearings, the defendant (or delinquent) has nothing to bargain with. Even if children did not actually use their rights in court, the very existence of those rights is useful to the extent that they affect the outcome of the case.

Another advantage to criminal court is that most crimes carry maximum sentences. Some states use indeterminate sentencing; that is, they leave the judgment of how soon to release a prisoner to the parole board rather than requiring release by a particular date which is set in advance by the judge. This is very much like what happens to juveniles, and it represents no particular advantage over the juvenile court system. For those children who are committed to institutions by the juvenile court for custody are usually committed until the age of majority (unless the court should decide to release them sooner). In other words, a child of fourteen faces a maximum sentence of seven years for being a delinquent, no matter what "crime" he or she may actually have committed. We saw this in its most disastrous form in the cause of Gerald Gault, but that was no freak happening. Although most juveniles who come before the children's courts do not end up spending their adolescent years in institutions, those who do would probably fare better if they had fixed terms which were *at least* no longer than those adults would receive for the same acts.

The final point I want to make about the relative merits of juvenile justice in theory and adult criminal courts in practice is that the extension of the full rights of the adversarial model of justice to children does not require any judge to treat children more severely than they are being treated now. An end to the juvenile court system would not require anyone to put children in adult prisons. Since there is no right to go to jail, children would not have their rights violated if they were not sent there. Judges cannot blame the adversarial system for their own sentencing decisions. Furthermore, there is nothing in the proposal to do away with juvenile courts which would prevent the current practices of diversion. Diversion is the attempt to deal with children's problems in social institutions other than courts. Instead of having a hearing, a child may be turned over to a school, a welfare agency, a youth organization, or a community group for guidance or a resolution of a problem. Such organizations do not have a court's authority over the child, and the hope is that the problem can be cleared up without stigmatizing the child as a delinquent. Setting aside the question of whether diversion reduces delinquency, we should notice that the practice may continue whether the child is being diverted from juvenile court or criminal court. Extra-legal methods of dealing with the unsocial behavior of children cannot be used to perpetuate a double standard in the law.

By now it should be clear that children do not get a better deal in juvenile court either in terms of procedures or in terms of respect. If they do get a better deal at sentencing time (which is doubtful), it is because the judges are more lenient, and not because the children have fewer rights. The abolition of the double standard before the court would in no way require judges to sentence people more strictly than they do now. We do not need to maintain the juvenile justice system today because judges in the nineteenth century hanged children from time to time.

There are serious questions about juvenile crime and youthful rebelliousness, and I do not mean to minimize them by rejecting the traditional solution. Some recent critics of the juvenile court system have advocated toleration and non-intervention as an alternative:

The conception of delinquency prevention, being ill conceived and devoid of demonstrable results, should be abandoned. . . . It must be effectively seen that all children engage in deviance, and that they become deviants through contingencies, complaints, and decisions of human beings with some authority. The things which have been called delinquency are with a small exceptionable portion normal problems of socialization, and should be so conceived. From such a view all children are delinquency prone and at the same time none are, hence such invidious terms are bereft of their meaning and should be discarded.[11]

The insight of this suggestion is that it reframes the problem. Instead of asking how to deal with delinquents, we should ask how to deal with the problems of socalizing children. That is, how are we to raise children to be admirable adults? It seems to me that, in general—but also especially in difficult cases—it is important to establish respect between children and the adult world.

Throughout this book I have advocated equal rights for children on the grounds that justice requires it. And one good way to show respect for people is to treat them justly. But beyond that, treating children justly means putting ourselves at their service at particular times and for particular purposes. It means having obligations to them when they are ready to make their demands on us. Sometimes, at least, when rights are at stake, we ought to be acting as children's agents rather than as their supervisors. I am not saying that children never need to be supervised, but if they are always and only supervised, the lesson they will learn is powerlessness—either as a fact of life, or as what we value in them.

Agency is a relationship which is based on a rather different picture of how children best become adults. Agents are sought out and respected for their acknowledged skills and abilities. There is nothing demeaning about being an agent, for it indicates a level of expertise which is not held by those seeking the services. Yet the authority of that expertise is conditional as long as the child retains the ultimate choice of agents. The ultimate control over the situation—though not the details—makes the agent's authority easier to accept, and provides the conditions for mutual respect and cooperation which do not exist easily in a strictly supervisory situation.

What I have just described is an ideal situation, of course. Adults do not often relate to their agents in this way, and some agents would prefer to be supervisors. Indeed, they sometimes try to infantilize their clients by keeping them ignorant or by making dismissal of the agent too costly. These are problems of institutional design, and they will not be overcome easily. But people who are interested in protecting children's rights should at least be able to see where they are headed. In the juvenile justice system, supervision is the wrong model. So is leaving children to their own devices. At least when it comes to rights, adults should be thinking about how to help children exercise them until such help is no longer needed. I would not even suggest that this amounts to a solution to the problem of juvenile crime, but after almost eighty years of juvenile justice, it seems to be an eminently more sensible course of action.

CHAPTER X

Rights of Privacy

The lack of privacy is a rather painful and almost pervasive fact of life for most children. A child's personal possessions are not safe from inspections by parents at home, teachers and other officials at school, or the police on the streets. Pockets, drawers, desks, rooms, lockers, automobile trunks, and other personal spaces which are all but sacrosanct in the adult world are, for children, open and available to sufficiently curious adults. Such invasions of privacy are established in custom, and usually sanctioned in law as well. Agents of the state are often empowered to maintain files of personal, educational, medical and legal information on children, and to distribute that information as they see fit. Although this reality touches some children more than others, no children are very secure from such invasions of privacy.

To add insult to injury, these intrusions into children's lives are not regarded as violations of right. Similar treatment of adults would quite properly raise a storm of protest that civil and human rights were being violated. But children are not thought of as having any right to privacy at all. For them, privacy is, at best, a privilege enjoyed at the pleasure of adults. Should adults wish to revoke it, the child has no recourse.

An end to the double standard of privacy would have an immediate and substantial effect on the day-to-day relations among children and adults. In this respect, a right to privacy is somewhat different from the rights to political participation and equal treatment in court. The impact of the partcipation of children on the political process would surely come slowly as children became better organized and more savvy about political realities. A change in juvenile court practices would have an immediately beneficial effect—but on a relatively small number of children. But privacy would add new dimensions to the ways adults could treat children in the course of normal relationships; so equal treatment here would make children's rights everyone's business since everyone would be touched by it in one way or another. If a children's rights movement is to make any headway in institutionalizing changes in the way our society conceives of children, it will have to happen at this somewhat more personal and mundane level as well as at the level of basic social and political structure. For children, the right to privacy involves more than merely the extension of an adult luxury to their domain; it is a toe in the door to wider recognition of children as people to be respected.

In order to make the connection between having privacy and being respected a little clearer, we should look a bit at the varieties of privacy, for privacy is not one right, but a collection of vaguely similar ones. The rights to privacy are found in the common law, in the interpretation of the Constitution, and in various state and federal statutes. Needless to say, these are not strictly separate categories. The Constitution may encompass and reflect the common law, and statutes may codify the intent of either or both. Still, to enumerate the rights of privacy which adults presently enjoy, it is easiest to use these headings.

Rights which develop in the common law develop slowly, and often become rights only through hindsight. In other words, disputes and conflicts are brought before the courts and decided on a case-by-case basis. Eventually someone sees a principle which threads through a number of these cases and gives it clear expression. If the principle is accepted, it is used to decide other cases, and when it is widely enough recognized, it may become the basis of a right in the common law. This is pretty much the story of the right of privacy. Prior to the late nineteenth century, there was nothing in the law called the right of privacy, but in 1878 Judge Thomas Cooley, commenting in *The Elements of Torts*, identified a right of personal immunity as "The right to one's person may be said to be a right to be let alone."[1] Building on this statement and on a number of nineteenth century court cases, Warren and Brandeis argued in the famous and now classic "The Right to Privacy" (1890) that privacy was a separate, if unarticulated, principle with its own legal history.[2] They proceeded to sharpen and clarify the right, and their interpretation eventually became the basis of future court decisions which recognized a right of privacy under its own name. That common law right is now generally regarded as covering four areas:

1. Unjustifiable infringement on the solitude of the individual.
2. The exploitation of the personality for commercial purposes (being primarily the use of a name, picture or likeness for business or related purposes).
3. The placing of an individual in a false public light by a misrepresentation of his status or personality.
4. The public disclosure of essentially private facts or the rehashing of linen (dirty or otherwise) in open for all to see.[3]

Rights in these areas aim, in the first instance, at curbing the embarrassment and pain which result from excessive curiosity about how the wealthy, the notorious, and the famous lead their lives. Less obviously, but just as surely, these rights protect a person's correspondence, works of art, and trade secrets from being used without consent. The second area mentioned above makes it clear that the right of privacy is designed to protect the pocketbook as well as the psyche. Being famous, notorious, or wealthy is often "worth" something, and the common law right of privacy is used to protect that value by prohibiting anyone else from cashing in uninvited. In the common law, privacy has some of the characteristics of a property.

The Constitution, primarily in the Bill of Rights, protects a somewhat different set of privacies. The First Amendment, in the course of securing the right of expression, prevents the government from compelling the public disclosure of one's opinions and beliefs. It also prevents involuntary disclosure of an individual's membership in a group or association. The Third Amendment, not much used but there nonetheless, protects the privacy of a person's home by prohibiting the forced housing of troops in peacetime. The Fourth Amendment has been more significant for a right of privacy. It establishes security against unreasonable search and seizure by the government, and, as such, is the main element in the limitation of citizen surveillance by police and social service agencies. The Fifth Amendment protects against self-incrimination, and thereby protects an individual's beliefs and opinions—at least in the context of an actual or potential legal proceeding.

The various privacies which are protected by the Constitution have the character of individual liberties. Yet according to Alan Westin, these very same amendments were interpreted between 1880 and 1937 as protecting "propertied privacy." That is, they protected business from governmental interference or regulation. Only recently did the privacy of persons and groups come again to dominate the interpretation of these rights.[4] The most significant case for a constitutional right of privacy to date is *Griswold vs. Connecticut*, which invalidated a Connecticut law forbidding dissemination of birth-control information. According to the court, the Constitution protects "zones of privacy," including marital privacy under the various guarantees of Amendments One, Three, Four, Five and Nine. Beyond the idea of "zones of privacy," what was new here was the citation of the Ninth Amendment which says that people may have rights which are not specifically mentioned in the Constitution. Some of the justices thought that privacy is one of these rights— and that it is so "fundamental" that states would be depriving their citizens of liberty or property without due process of law if they did not make room for a right to privacy.[5] This argument takes the long way around with the right to privacy, but the upshot is to protect that right—however it is interpreted— against laws which would limit or undermine it.

Pretty clearly a Constitutional right to "zones of privacy" is sufficiently vague so as not to inspire much confidence about exactly what is private and what is not. Privacy rights which are specified in statutes tend to be more specific and easier to enumerate. By statute we have the right not to have our mail opened, the right to confidentiality from lawyers, doctors, and clergy, the right to refuse a lie-detector test as a condition of employment, and the right to prevent some information about ourselves from being handed out to whoever asks for it. There is no easy way to list all of a person's statutory rights to privacy. Some of these rights, like the Privacy Act of 1974, protect us against the federal government, but not against the states or private institutions. Others, like the right to refuse a lie-detector test, are statutes in some states only. Furthermore, state laws about what information is confidential and who is excluded from the circle of confidentiality differ widely. On top of that, this is an area of law which is presently undergoing substantial change as people are becoming more sensitive to the potential consequences of information-gathering and data banks for personal privacy. But my purpose here is not to come up with a list of privacy rights. The point is that these various rights presently enjoyed by adults are not, for the most part, extended to children. This double standard, too, should be abolished, and again, its abolition would probably be of benefit to society on the whole.

So far I have been describing in a general way what the rights to privacy are—at least in their present form—but I have not said much about why people should have privacy as a right. That is, what is it about privacy that makes it worth protecting in this way? This is an important question for our purposes since we need to decide whether the reasons we value privacy for ourselves are reasons we should value it for children as well. For only if some of these reasons do not really apply to children will it be possible to make a case for the double standard. Otherwise, we should protect their privacy to the same extent as we would anyone else's.

There are three basic kinds of reasons which are usually given to defend or extend the rights to privacy. The first is that a right to privacy sets limits on those areas of life which are open to direct intrusion by the most powerful public institution —the state. The point here is to maintain a certain amount of institutional diversity in the society; to encourage the coexistence of different forms of social life and to prevent the state from imposing a homogeneous way of living on its citizenry. The second reason for a right to privacy is that intrusions on privacy are, by nature, indignities. To violate a person's privacy without consent, even if that privacy was not worth much to the person at the time, is to treat that person with disrespect. The third basis for a right of privacy is that privacy itself is of value—either monetary or psychic—to many people, either for its own sake or as a means to other ends. Let us look a little more closely at each of these reasons to see whether and to what extent they are reasons to extend privacy rights to children.

Some privacy rights are aimed specifically at limiting intrusions by the state as opposed to intrusions by private organizations such as business, advertising agencies, credit bureaus, churches, and charities. The Constitutional rights prohibiting unreasonable search and seizure and self-incrimination are prime examples here, as is the Privacy Act of 1974. It is not intrusions *per se* which are ruled out, and there is no suggestion that what remains private is of any intrinsic value. As a matter of fact, the privacies protected by the search and seizure prohibitions are more often than not regarded as harmful, disgusting, or a waste of time by the general public. For citizens may use their privacy to conspire to commit crimes or to indulge in obscene books and films if they so desire. Nevertheless, we make a judgment that less harm will come from allowing these "private" activities than from allowing the state to put a stop to them. We think that a state which engaged in the extensive surveillance required to suppress these activities would not be a very satisfactory place to live. For such a state would be able to suppress activities which were merely unusual or idiosyncratic as well as those which were genuinely harmful.

The Privacy Act is also best understood in terms of the idea that the power of surveillance which the state has over its citizenry should be limited. This act applies only to the records of federal agencies, and it does not severely restrict access to those records. But to the extent that it limits access at all, it does so from a sense that the power of personal information in the hands of government is a substantial source of social control. This law establishes certain rights for individuals against agencies. The agencies must make public a description of the records they keep, they must disclose the contents to the subjects of the information upon demand, and they must make some efforts to keep the information accurate. More to our point, the law restricts access to the records outside the agency (although it does not absolutely prevent others from having them), and requires that agencies keep their records secure. It also places some limits on information-gathering, and takes some steps toward preventing the Social Security number from becoming a universal identifier.[6]

Despite the fact that the law is sufficiently flexible that none of us should sleep very much better because of it, it is motivated by a sense that information is powerful, and the lack of it places certain limitations on the possibilities of controlling citizen behavior. The law does address the issue of accuracy of information, and that is not a privacy issue; but it goes beyond concern for accuracy by acknowledging that even a correct file could be of harm to someone in the wrong hands. And this harm is more significant to us than the possible benefits of the unchecked possession of the truth by the state.

I have labored this rationale for privacy somewhat because we tend to ignore it in situations where the state is dealing with children. Prior to the *Gault* decision, courts were able to take great liberties with children's privacy. Children now have the right not to incriminate themselves in court, but they are still not able to demand protection against unreasonable search and seizure. In effect, this means that the state in the person of the police officer is unchecked in intrusions into a child's privacy. Furthermore, employees of public schools—the major state institution in the lives of children—are not prevented in any way from invading the privacy of students. Teachers and administrators may inspect lockers, desks, papers, personal correspondence, and pockets without a search warrant and without probable cause. They may gather intellectual, medical, and economic information about students and pass it on to anyone they choose. Not only do students have no control over their files, often they may not even see them, even with parental permission. Is there any justification for treating children differently from adults *vis à vis* the state in these circumstances?

On the surface it would seem that if we are concerned with limiting the power of the state in certain respects, we should want it limited in the face of all individuals—not merely some. This is, again, partly a question of social justice. Once we recognize the dangers of unlimited state surveillance, and the benefits to be derived by individuals from avoiding it, it is unjust to concentrate those benefits in the hands of some members of the society at the expense of others. It means that those without privacy and a chance to work out their own life patterns are paying for the opportunities of others. Beyond the issue of social justice here is the matter of self-interest. If we allow the state to intrude on the privacy of some but not others, the basis of the intrusion undermines the principle of limited government. For the implication is that the state can violate a citizen's privacy in principle although it may choose not to for a large number of citizens for practical reasons. However, practicalities can change, and if the state should step up surveillance of adults, it will not seem like the serious violation of principle that it is. So the basis of my privacy is weakened when the state may intrude on a child's privacy. Still, if the difference between children and adults were strikingly clear in ways relevant to this reason for privacy, there might be no injustice or no danger to adults in the violations of the privacy of children.

One difference which cannot be appealed to here is a difference in the likelihood of a responsible use of the privacy. It is entirely possible that children who are not interfered with by the state will behave in rather irresponsible ways under the umbrella of privacy. But remember that admittedly irresponsible behavior in adults is *precisely* what is being protected here as well. Adults have a right to privately plan crimes, use dangerous drugs, view obscene pictures, engage in disapproved sexual acts, and so on. In light of this it is more than a little hypocritical to say that children should not have such privacy because they will use it irresponsibly. Anyway, this argument misses the point of the rationale for protecting privacy against the state. The problem is with state power and its effect on social and cultural life. Whether it is children or adults who engage in questionable activities, we have made the judgment that it would be better to deal with them through some mechanism other than the state. And this judgment should have nothing to do with the age of the citizen.

The other argument for seeing a difference between children and adults with respect to these kinds of intrusions of privacy is that the state sometimes acts in the capacity of a parent—

especially in school and in court. (We discussed the concept of *parens patriae* in Chapter IX.) The best that can be said for that argument here is that it runs headlong into conflict with the basic conception of limited government. The aim of privacy under this heading is to mark a distinction between state institutions and private ones so as to foster and encourage diversity in cultural life. To make the state a parent—not for the purposes of custody, but for the purposes of surveillance and control— is to collapse the distinction and to take back with one hand what was given with the other. For where are we supposed to develop this diversity if the public schools are unchecked in their power to intrude on students' privacy? If ever there was a danger to homogeneous culture, that is it. This is not a criticism of public education, but of education in an institution which is unchecked in its power to demand conformity in all areas of action and belief. Adults do not give up their civil and constitutional rights when they go to school, and children should not be made to, either.

We have been dealing with privacies, so far, which are rights primarily because we want a check on the power of the state. There are, of course, other reasons to have these rights. A second has to do with the indignity which accompanies many invasions of privacy. Uninvited prying and snooping into another's life is demeaning to that person and signifies disrespect in addition to any pain or embarrassment it may cause.

A concern for the dignity of the individual is surely behind the development of the common law protection of the individual's psyche as well as her or his body from assault or invasion by others, and this also seems to be much of the motivation behind the Warren and Brandeis analysis of the right to privacy. Here the protection is not primarily against the state, but against other members of the society. Although a person cannot expect to keep everything secret, some personal information is likely to be demeaning when openly discussed by others. This includes information about the unmentionables—excretion and sexuality, detailed discussion of personal habits, gossip about personal relationships when broadcast sufficiently widely, medical histories, and other facts that tend to stigmatize. In the interests of dignity, the law grants people a right to recover for sufficiently debasing intrusions of these privacies. Children, however, do not have equal access to civil courts. Yet even if they did, they would have to prove that the invasion of privacy was demeaning to them. And adults do not generally concede that children have a sense of dignity in the first place. Are invasions of children's privacy really so damaging to them?

The problem with a good deal of the thinking about children on this question is that people tend to ignore the differences between a person's sense of dignity and their dignity. Since young children often do not have a well-developed sense of dignity, we tend to assume that it is impossible to do injury to their dignity. Aside from the fact that it ignores the indignities done to older children, it is simply not true. A person's sense of dignity has to do with his or her own perception of the ways in which others treat them. People who are not sufficiently aware of the differences between conventional, socially acceptable treatment on the one hand, and shabby treatment on the other, may not be able to perceive the occasions on which they are subjected to the latter. They may have no sense that what is being done to them is unusual or worse than what is done to others. Thus, they may feel no embarrassment, no affront, no injury in a situation which would wound a person with a more developed conception of dignity. This often happens to young children, and all the more when the indignities are subtle or a matter of tone rather than content.

Nevertheless, a person does not have to realize an indignity to suffer one. Dignity is more a matter of how a person is perceived by the rest of society than it is a matter of how a person perceives her or himself (although these are not entirely unrelated). I may be too thick to realize that I have been insulted on some occasion, but if others recognize the insult, my dignity has been diminished. So it is with children. Even when they do not object to shabby treatment—when they do not even realize that it is shabby—others who witness that treatment understand its significance. Their understanding is the main source of the indignity. When a child's privacy is invaded, the child may not understand this as an invasion. The child may not know what the norms of social behavior for adults regarding privacy actually are. Still, the rest of us know; and we know that we would not stand for such treatment ourselves because it is demeaning.

The point is that the privacies which protect a person's dignity protect it whether the person appreciates the fact or not. Children are no less injured by invasions of privacy than adults from the point of view of the rest of society, although they may feel less pain for failure to realize the insult. Age and understanding have little to do with this rationale for a right to privacy. If it is a good reason to protect the privacy of adults, it should apply to children as well.

This brings us now to the third rationale for the rights to privacy. Privacy itself is of value to people either for its own sake, or as a means to other ends. This value may be psychic or monetary, and we should consider these possibilities separately.

Privacy is not of identical or even of equal value to everyone. And it is not the sort of thing which most people pursue without limit. Hermits and recluses value extensive isolation, but the rest of us like to pick our own private moments. We want to exercise the rights to privacy when we want and need them, for at those times privacy can be of considerable value to us. The value is partly psychological; privacy can be of benefit to our mental lives. In the first place, some people sometimes value aloneness or seclusion just for its own sake. They don't want to be alone in order to do anything—they just want to be alone. Perhaps it feels better. At any rate, a right to privacy which forbids trespass can make this condition possible.

More typically, privacy is treated as a means to other psychic satisfactions, desires, or needs. For example, people may value seclusion because it helps them to reflect about things and understand them better. Some people need to be alone in order to relax or in order to rejuvenate themselves for the continuation of life's business. Privacy may not be the only condition under which it is possible to reflect or relax, but it is a pretty effective means to those ends for most people, and that is a good reason to value its protection. Privacy can also create safe conditions for personal experimentation. Zones of privacy are handy places to polish one's skills before going public. People learn to swim or dance or read aloud in private partly because the thought of doing so in public is too awesome. Without the right to privacy, if it were permissible to record and publicly display these attempts, many such activities would simply not be attempted. Privacy is also a means to security. The idea that there are places and times which are secure from the intrusion of others gives some people peace of mind. This sort of security has always been counted among the chief advantages of organized society. Finally, privacy as a right of the confidentiality of others is a means to the uninhibited exploration of beliefs or of possible courses of action. A person may raise information with a doctor, lawyer, or a clergyman which could be damaging as public knowledge, but which is important for having accurate advice about what to do. It is just because people are not expected to "go it alone" in difficult situations that a right to privacy understood in this way is so valuable.

Over and above its psychological value, privacy plays a role in certain economic transactions and so has a monetary use to people as well. Limitations on prying and snooping protect more than dignity—they protect trade secrets as well. Such secrets can be worth money if nobody else has them (as is the formula for Coca-Cola); but they can also be of value if others must pay for their use. Privacy is at the bottom of the laws concerning copyright and royalties. The common law right of privacy is also the means by which well-known people make money from product endorsements. Even if Bruce Jenner ate Wheaties, one cannot now say so in print without paying for the privilege. For the rest of us, there are times when personal information is worth something undisclosed. A history of psychiatric care could keep a person out of a job for which she was otherwise qualified. The privacy of the record might be crucial in such a case. There is a substantial amount of information which is used to rank people in ways that have economic consequences. Reports from teachers, former employers, credit investigators, doctors, and social service agencies—to say nothing of the police. Some of this information may be relevant in the determination of who gets what jobs or other social benefits, but much of what is used to make these decisions is not strictly relevant. To the extent that the rights to privacy are being violated in such circumstances, these violations are not just embarrassing; they are expensive.

And what of children? Are they in a position to reap the psychic and monetary benefits of privacy? For the most part, the answer is "yes" and that is because private means "non-public" more often than it means "alone." The only area in which privacy may not be of use to children (young children, anyway) is the area of the psychological value of seclusion as a means to other social ends. Young children may well not know how to use seclusion for reflection, relaxation, or rejuvenation. And, of course, nobody can literally help them with this, since the helping would destroy the seclusion. But this does not mean that children—even very young children—cannot sometimes enjoy seclusion for its own sake. Nor does it mean that children can derive no social benefit from other forms of privacy. The word "private" does not apply to individuals alone. Confidentiality, which is an extremely important form of privacy, requires a relationship which involves more than one person. The relationship is "private" because it is severely limited to a small circle of people and because the person with the privacy has control over the communications. This conception of privacy accords well with our conception of borrowed capacities and child agency.

Once the relationship between child and child agent is protected as confidential, there is no rationale for protecting the privacy rights of adults which do not also apply to children. Even seclusion should be available to them as a right, for children might find it useful for its own sake even before they can use it as a means to other social goods. To extend to children the right of privacy is not to leave them alone or abandon them to themselves. Growing up requires room to experiment and room to confide in people who can offer uninhibited advice. It also requires enough dignity to shore up the occasional crises in self-confidence. These are some of the more important benefits of a right to privacy for adults, and children may be in more urgent need of them. If children are to begin reaping these benefits in our society, it seems most likely to me that they will need the service of agents. If what I've had to say here has been thorough enough, it should seem most likely to the reader as well.

CHAPTER XI

Concluding Remarks

In these chapters I have tried to develop a firm base on which to ground rethinking our relationships to children. If we are to seriously address the problems of child abuse and child neglect, then we must face them in their whole social context and not merely as isolated phenomenon. We must decide how we want to live with children; and this will take us well beyond deciding how to identify and respond to their ill-treatment. For the last three hundred years or so child protection has guided our thought and our policies about children. Child protection, however, has run its course. It is no longer adequate to meet the needs of children and adults in the business of getting on with life in a humane and dignified way.

The failure of child protection is twofold. First, it does not meet the requirements of fairness. Children are denied some of the benefits and advantages of social life which are available to adults. Children could enjoy these benefits, but we withhold them in the name of child protection—even when there are possible ways to extend them. Second, as a practical matter, child protection has been too easy to acknowledge in theory and to ignore in fact. "Protected" children have been too easily damaged for us to have much confidence in state paternalism.

As laudable as the caretaker approach may seem, and as valuable as it was in combating child abuse and child neglect in earlier times, it has its weaknesses. Two of its principal problems are that it does not really come to grips with the fact that parents do have an interest in their children which may conflict with developing them into independent adults, and also that it does not make it very clear why the state should be a better caretaker than a parent when it assumes that role. The caretaker approach does not provide the necessary concepts for expressing these problems, and so tends to ignore them— or dismiss them as abnormalities. But they are real problems, and persistent ones. They have been around as long as child protection and they are still around today.

Even after parents began to take a more child-oriented view of childrearing in the seventeenth century, they continued to have an interest in their children which went well beyond caretaking—and sometimes came into conflict with it. A good deal of this interest was economic in nature. In the first place, people with wealth continued to have a concern for lineage and the continuity of the family name. They had their estate their property and social standing—from their ancestors, and were well aware of the fact that they would be passing it on to their children. Such parents had an interest in their children's ability and desire to improve the estate, whether or not the children shared that interest. The child who forsakes the family enterprise for opportunity and adventure may leave his parents wondering how that decision will transform the family wealth. These conflicts are still well-known today. And they really are conflicts.

The economic interests that the poor had in their children were no less acute. Depending on the economic arrangements of any given society, children are bound to be either an asset or a liability to their parents. This can be calculated by comparing the cost of supporting them to the benefits of having them. The benefits in our society are no longer economic, but that was not so in the past. A poor family had a very great interest in putting its children to work. The survival of the family unit often depended on it. But since children were not officially recognized as their parents' commodities, the resolutions of these conflicts had to be couched in the language of protection and the best interests of the child.

This is precisely what happened in nineteenth century

America. Protective legislation, particularly in the areas of child labor and compulsory education, in effect limited the extent to which children could be treated as parental property. To this extent it is well-grounded in the caretaker approach. But the assumptions about a harmony of interests within the family implicit in this outlook were just not very realistic. The presumption that "fit" parents would prefer to have their children in school than in the fields or in the mills encouraged the belief that the poor were often unfit parents. The economic reality of the life of poverty was largely ignored in favor of the belief that parents who did not put the welfare of their children first must be ignorant or drunkards. In this way child protection allowed child advocates to avoid the social conditions of child abuse and neglect, and treat it simply as a moral problem. Since the approach made no provisions for a conflict of interest between parents and children, it did not arm its proponents with the concepts they would need to deal adequately with those problems.

The preferred solution of removing children from abusive parents could only make sense as long as one believed that the abuse was an abnormality—a moral monstrosity of rare occurrence. To see it instead as a more or less pervasive conflict of interest between parents and children would require solutions on a much more grand scale. Nobody in the child protection field seriously contemplated the wholesale rescue of the children of the poor. They worked on a case-by-case basis, taking satisfaction in saving trees without thinking too much about the size of the forest. The state built institutions to house "rescued" children, and so entered the parenting business itself, but these institutions were always intended to serve the few worst cases. As far as the state was concerned, there was a clear difference between the worst and the rest. The honorable poor took care of their children and respected their right to protection. The unfit parents who failed in this respect forfeited their children to the state which, acting as a parent, would provide the quality of care every child had a right to.

Perhaps if the state had made good on its promise to provide quality child care, there would have been little to complain about in the child protection ideology. But, in fact, that has not been the case. State institutions for juveniles quickly became custodial rather than educational or "rehabilitative." Actually, they are worse than custodial. In investigation after investigation they have been exposed and denounced as dangerous, destructive, abusive places. The rhetoric of protection of children has turned into a rhetoric of the protection of society from the dangerous inmates who are the products of these places. Other areas in which the state has done a poor job at child protection are not so spectacular, but equally troubling. The practice of foster care placements of children who are separated from their parents is generally acknowledged to suffer from an endemic disruption and discontinuity in the children's lives. Foster children tend to be moved from home to home, and with each move the question of how much they are to see their biological parents may be raised again. The unsettling effects of these practices tend to undermine the quality of the childhood experience. The problems with that other state institution of child care —the public school—are also well known. The state, acting *in loco parentis*, by and large favors strict discipline and heavy-handed authoritarianism. But what is worse, a substantial number of observers have come to wonder whether there is much quality to the education. These questions were raised sharply in the context of the Alternative Schools of the late 1960's and 1970's. In short, the state has not proven itself to be a fit parent where the biological parents have failed. It has not protected the children in its care in ways that we can feel very comfortable about.

Here, too, the difficulties have their roots in certain inadequacies of the child-protection ideology. The government stepped into the role of child-protector without giving much thought to the question of how a state differed from a parent. This should not surprise us too much for, in the first place, the state only acknowledged a responsibility to children as a last resort. That is, when parents failed, that state would intercede. This sort of intervention requires *only a transfer* of responsibilities. It does not do anything to alter traditional parent-child relationships. Secondly, the ideology encourages us to see parents in a single dimension—as protectors of children. No other role is considered, so no other role is regarded as appropriate for a government which acts as a parent. Under the extreme circumstances of the worse cases of child abuse, it was easiest for believers in the caretaker ideology to respond to the failure of child protection with a larger dose of the same medicine.

Nan Berger sums up the problem with this governmental attitude in her criticism of the approach of (English) law relating to children:

> The State, when it took children away from parents, assumed the same rights over them as their parents had.
>
> Little if anything in subsequent Children's Acts has altered this situation and you can search through existing legislation as it affects children and not find a single sentence which enhances the dignity of childhood or recognizes that children are people in their own right and not just appendages of adults. Where parental authority has been restricted as being unreasonably oppressive through cruelty and neglect, the State has taken over and given the child some protection. It has not added to the child's freedom or status.[1]

Child protection has been concerned with the quality of care of the child, and therefore with the fitness of the caretaker. It has not been concerned with fundamental questions about the nature and limits of adult authority over children. It is the sense that the ways in which adults control children and make decisions for them are themselves a part of the mistreatment and oppression of children which is absent from the ideology, and is ignored by the government when it becomes involved.

None of this adds up to a guarantee that we can improve the lot of children in our society by thinking in terms of equal rights. Still, it should be more than enough to clarify the need and provide the incentive for pursuing social policies which acknowledge children's rights. Instead of devising new ways to protect children we can begin to ask ourselves how to extend rights to them. This can be done in any area of life which includes or affects children.

Our preferred solution to any problem should involve bringing children out of protective isolation and treating them to the greatest possible extent as we treat adults. To do this we must ask what capacities adults use to exercise their rights when faced with similar problems. Should children lack those capacities, we may go on to explore whether they are the sort that can be borrowed and whether it is possible to establish agents to loan them. Detailed answers to these questions will help us design solutions which respect children and strengthen their position in American society. While it is clear that this approach to children's policy does not yet have a track record, and so has not been put to a practical test, it offers us a chance to improve on a fairly sorry state of affairs. To the extent that it is possible to think such matters out in advance, equal rights for children is a decent bet. Our children really can't wait much longer.

Notes

Notes

Notes

INTRODUCTION

1. William K. Frankena, "Some Beliefs about Justice," in Joel Feinberg and Hyman Gross (eds.), *Justice: Selected Readings* (Belmont, Ca: Dickenson Publishing Co., 1977), p. 48.

CHAPTER I

1. "The Failure to Intercede," *Minor Affairs* (Lincoln, Massachusetts, December, 1978), p. 2.
2. *Boston Globe* (November 21, 1978), p. 14.
3. John Locke, *Second Treatise of Government* (Indianapolis: Bobbs-Merrill Co., 1952), p. 33.
4. Kenneth Keniston, "Change the Victims—Or the Society?," in Beatrice and Ronald Gross (eds.), *The Children's Rights Movement* (New York: Anchor Press, 1977), p. 232.
5. Richard Farson, *Birthrights* (New York: Macmillan, 1974), p. 1.
6. John Holt, *Escape from Childhood* (New York: E. P. Dutton, 1974), p. 1.
7. Farson, *op. cit.*, p. 9.
8. Richard Farson, "A Child's Bill of Rights," in Gross and Gross, *op. cit.*, pp. 325–28.

CHAPTER III

1. "United Nations Declaration of the Rights of the Child," in Gross and Gross, *op. cit.*, pp. 336–336.

2. These documents and Hart's essay are reprinted in A. I. Melden (ed.), *Human Rights* (Belmont, Ca: Wadsworth, 1970). Feinberg's discussion of human rights is in Joel Feinberg, *Social Philosophy* (Englewood Cliffs, N.J.: Prentice-Hall, Inc., 1973), Chapter 6.
3. Jeremy Bentham, "Anarchical Fallacies," in Melden, *op cit.*, p. 31.
4. *Ibid.*, p. 32.
5. Christopher Hill, *The Century of Revolution* (New York: W. W. Norton Co., Inc., 1961), p. 66.
6. Herbert Morris, "Persons and Punishment" in Joel Feinberg and Hyman Gross, (eds.) *Punishment* (Belmont, Ca: Dickenson, 1975), p. 83.

CHAPTER IV

1. In many societies, people also have moral rights which are not established in law. That means, of course, that such rights are not enforceable in courts, but to the extent that there are informal mechanisms such as community pressure, these rights may be no less effective for that.
2. Kenneth Boulding, "Social Justice in Social Dynamics," in Richard B. Brandt, *Social Justice* (Englewood Cliffs, N.J.: Prentice-Hall, Inc., 1962), p. 83.
3. Joel Feinberg, *op. cit.*, p. 99.
4. Frankena, *op. cit.*, p. 48.

CHAPTER V

1. Using the skills of others is a notion which Jane R. Martin develops in her lecture "Basic Education, Or How to Preserve the *Status Quo* Without Really Trying," delivered at the Harvard Graduate School of Education, May 1976, and at Rollins College, January 1977. She proposed that cooperatives in the 3R's be formed in which skill and knowledge of the 3R's are shared. Jane R. Martin, Department of Philosophy, University of Massachusetts-Boston, Boston, Mass.
2. Francis Schrag, "The Child's Status in a Democratic State," *Political Theory*, Vol. 3, No. 4 (1975), p. 449.
3. Lorenne M. G. Clark, "Privacy, Property, Freedom and the Family," in R. Bronaugh (ed.), *The Philosophy of Law* (Westport, Conn.: Greenwood Press, 1978), p. 168.
4. Isaiah Berlin, *Four Essays on Liberty* (London: Oxford Press, 1969), p. 123.

5. H. L. A. Hart, "Are There Any Natural Rights?" in A. I. Melden (ed.), *Human Rights* (Belmont, Ca. Wadsworth, 1970), p. 64.
6. John Stuart Mill, *On Liberty* (Indianapolis: Bobbs-Merrill Co., 1956), p. 13.
7. Mill, *op. cit.*, p. 14.
8. *Ibid.*
9. Gerald Dworkin, "Paternalism," in Richard A. Wasserstrom, (ed.), *Morality and the Law* (Belmont, Ca: Wadsworth, 1971), p. 108.

CHAPTER VI

1. Aleksander W. Rudzinski, "The Duty to Rescue: A Comparative Analysis," in James M. Ratcliffe (ed.), *The Good Samaritan and the Law* (Garden City, New York: Anchor Books, 1966), pp. 91–134.

CHAPTER VII

1. Ronald Dworkin, *Taking Rights Seriously* (Cambridge, Mass.: Harvard University Press, 1977), pp. 188–89.
2. Kenneth Keniston, *All Our Children* (New York: Harcourt, Brace and Jovanovich, 1977), p. 17.

CHAPTER VIII

1. Ronald Dworkin, *op. cit.*, p. 269.
2. *Ibid.*, p. 191.
3. Carl Cohen, *Democracy* (Athens, Ga.: University of Georgia Press, 1971), p. 41.
4. *Ibid.*, p. 49.
5. *Ibid.*, p. 50.
6. Carl Cohen, "On the Child's Status in the Democratic State," *Political Theory*, Vol. 3, No. 4 (Nov. 1975), p. 460.
7. R. W. Connell, *The Child's Construction of Politics* (Carlton, Victoria: Melbourne University Press, 1971), p. 35.
8. Clyde Evans, "Children's Rights: The Incompetence Objection," unpublished manuscript, p. 19. Clyde Evans, Department of Philosophy, University of Massachusetts-Boston, Boston, Mass.

9. Carole Pateman, *Participation and Democratic Theory* (Cambridge, Eng.: Cambridge University Press, 1970), p. 42.
10. G. B. Shaw, "Parents and Children," *Misalliance* (New York: Brentano's, 1914), p. cxxi.

CHAPTER IX

1. *Juvenile Court Judges Journal*, quoted in W. Vaughn Stapleton and Lee E. Teitlebaum, *In Defense of Youth* (New York: Russell Sage Foundation, 1972), p. 35.
2. *Laws of Illinois*, quoted in Hon. Richard S. Tuthill, "History of the Children's Court in Chicago," *Children's Courts in the United States* (Washington, D.C.: Government Printing Office, 1904), p. 2.
3. *Laws of Illinois*, quoted in Stapleton and Teitlebaum, *op. cit.*, p. 22.
4. Lois G. Forer, *"No One Will Lissen"* (New York: Grosset and Dunlap, 1970), pp. 67–105.
5. Hon. Ben B. Lindsey, "The Juvenile Court of Denver," *Children's Courts in the United States*, *op. cit.*, p. 29.
6. *Ibid.*, p. 30.
7. *In re Gault*, in Frederic L. Faust and Paul J. Brantingham (eds.), *Juvenile Justice Philosophy* (St. Paul, Minn.: West Publishing Co., 1974).
8. Stapleton and Teitlebaum, *op. cit.*, pp. 32–37.
9. Forer, *op. cit.*, p. 41.
10. *In re Gault*, Faust and Brantingham, *op. cit.*, pp. 360–420.
11. Edwin M. Lenert, *Instead of Court* (Washington, D.C.: Government Printing Office, 1971), p. 91.

CHAPTER X

1. Thomas Cooley, *The Elements of Torts*, in Morris Ernst and Alan Schwartz, *Privacy: The Right to Be Let Alone* (London: MacGibbon and Kee, 1968), p. 49.
2. Warren and Brandeis, "The Right to Privacy," reprinted in Alan Breckenridge, *The Right to Privacy* (Lincoln, Nb.: University of Nebraska Press, 1970).
3. Michael Mayer, *Rights of Privacy* (New York: Law-Arts Publishers, Inc., 1972), p. 5.
4. Alan Westin, *Privacy and Freedom* (New York: Atheneum, 1967), pp. 330–42.
5. *Ibid.*, p. 353.

6. Kent Greenawalt, *Legal Protections of Privacy* (Washington, D.C.: Government Printing Office, 1975).

CHAPTER XI

1. Nan Berger, "The Child, the Law, and the State," in Adams, *et al., Children's Rights* (New York: Praeger, 1972), p. 163.

Bibliography

Bibliography

CHILDREN'S RIGHTS

ADAMS, Paul, et al., *Children's Rights: Toward the Liberation of the Child*, New York: Praeger, 1972.

BANDMAN, B., "Do Children Have Natural Rights?," *Philosophy of Education; Proceedings of the 29th Annual Meeting*, 1973.

BURT, Robert A., "Developing Constitutional Rights of, in and for Children," in Margaret L. Rosenheim (ed.), *Pursuing Justice for the Child*, Chicago: University of Chicago Press, 1976.

FARSON, Richard, *Birthrights*, New York: Macmillan, 1974.

GROSS, Beatrice and Richard Gross (eds.), *The Children's Rights Movement*, New York: Anchor Press, 1977.

HAFEN, Bruce C., "Children's Liberation and the New Egalitarianism: Some Reservations About Abandoning Youth to Their Rights," *Brigham Young Law Review*, v.1976, n.3., 1976.

HOLT, John, *Escape from Childhood*, New York: E. P. Dutton, 1974.

KLEINIG, John, "Mill, Children and Rights," *Educational Philosophy and Theory*, v.8, n.1., 1976.

MARKER, Gail and Paul R. Friedman, "Rethinking Children's Rights," *Children Today*, Nov.-Dec., 1973.

SHAW, G. B., "Parents and Children," *Misalliance*, New York: Brentano's, 1914.

WILKERSON, Albert E. (ed.), *The Rights of Children*, Philadelphia: Temple University Press, 1973.

WORSFELD, Victor L., "A Philosophical Justification of Children's Rights," *Harvard Educational Review*, v.44, n.1, 1974.

YOUNG, Robert, "Education and the 'Rights' of Adolescents," *Educational Philosophy and Theory*, v.8, n.1. 1976.

CHILDREN AND SOCIAL POLICY

BRONFENBRENNER, Urie, *Two Worlds of Childhood: U.S. and U.S.S.R.*, New York: Basic Books, 1970.

CLARK, Ted, *The Oppression of Youth*, New York: Harper & Row, 1975.

COHEN, Julius; Reginald A. H. Robson; Alan Bates, *Parental Authority: The Community and the Law*, New Brunswick, New Jersey: Rutgers University Press, 1958.

FRIEDENBERG, Edgar Z., *The Dignity of Youth and Other Atavisims*, Boston: Beacon Press, 1965.

GOLDSTEIN, Joseph; Anna Freud; and Albert J. Solnit, *Beyond the Best Interest of the Child*, New York: The Free Press, 1973.

GOODMAN, Paul, *Growing Up Absurd: Problems of Youth in the Organized System*, New York: Random House, 1960.

GOTTLIEB, David (ed.), *Children's Liberation*, Englewood Cliffs, N.J.: Prentice-Hall, 1973.

HYMAN, I. and K. Schreiber, "The School Psychologist as Child Advocate," *Children Today*, March-April, 1974.

JACKSON, Sonia, "The Children's Act 1975: Parent's Rights and Child Welfare," *British Journal of Law and Society*, v.3, n.1. 1976.

KENISTON, Kenneth, *All Our Children*, New York: Harcourt, Brace and Jovanovich, 1977.

MANDELL, Betty Reid, *Where Are the Children?*, Lexington, Mass.: Lexington Books, 1973.

MEAD, Margaret and Martha Wolfenstein (eds.), *Childhood in Contemporary Cultures*, Chicago: University of Chicago Press, 1955.

O'NEILL, Onora and William Ruddick (eds.), *Having Children*, New York: Oxford University Press, 1979.

SCHORR, Alvin (ed.), *Children and Decent People*, New York: Basic Books, 1974.

SENN, Milton, *Speaking Out for America's Children*, New Haven: Yale University Press, 1977.

SIDEL, Ruth, *Women and Childcare in China*, New York: Hill and Wang, 1972.

STEINER, Gilbert Y., *The Children's Cause*, Washington, D.C.: The Brookings Institution, 1976.

YOUTH LIBERATION OF ANN ARBOR, *Youth Liberation: News, Politics, and Survival Information*, Washington, N.J.: Times Change Press, 1972.

PHILOSOPHICAL WORKS ON RIGHTS

DWORKIN, Ronald, *Taking Rights Seriously*, Cambridge, Mass.: Harvard University Press, 1977.

FEINBERG, Joel, *Social Philosophy*, Englewood Cliffs, N.J.: Prentice-Hall, 1973.

LYONS, David (ed.), *Rights*, Belmont, Ca.: Wadsworth Publishing Co., 1979.

MACKLIN, Ruth, "Moral Concerns and Appeals to Rights and Duties," *Hastings Center Report*, October, 1976.

MELDEN, A. I. (ed.), *Human Rights*, Belmont, Ca.: Wadsworth Publishing Co., 1970.

HISTORICAL BACKGROUND ON CHILDREN

ALLEN, Anne, and Arthur Morton, *This Is Your Child*, London: Routledge and Kegan Paul,

ARIES, Philippe, *Centuries of Childhood*, New York: Random House, 1962.

BREMMER, Robert II. (ed.), *Children and Youth in America*, Cambridge, Mass.: Harvard University Press, 1970, 1971, 1974.

DEMAUSE, Lloyd (ed.), *The History of Childhood*, New York: Psychohistory Press, 1974.

HANDLIN, Oscar and Mary Handlin, *Facing Life*, Boston: Little Brown and Co., 1971.

HUNT, David, *Parents and Children in History*, New York: Basic Books, 1970.

LOCKE, John, *Second Treatise of Government*, New York: Bobbs-Merrill Co., 1952.

MIDDLETON, Nigel, *When Family Failed*, London: Victor Gollancz Ltd., 1971.

PLATT, Anthony M., *The Child Savers: The Invention of Delinquency*, Chicago: University of Chicago Press, 1969.

ROTHMAN, David J., *The Discovery of the Asylum*, Boston: Little Brown and Co., 1971.

ROUSSEAU, J. J., *Emile: or, Education*, New York: E. P. Dutton and Co., 1911.

SLATER, Peter Gregg, *Children in the New England Mind: In Death and in Life*, Hamden, Conn.: The Shoestring Press, Inc., 1977.

CHILDREN IN POLITICS

COHEN, Carl, *Democracy*, Athens, Ga.: University of Georgia Press, 1971.

————, "On the Children's Status in the Democratic State," *Political Theory*, v.3, n.4. 1975.

COHEN, Howard, "On the Exchange Between Schrag and Cohen, 'The Child's Status in the Democratic State'," *Political Theory*, v.6, n.2. 1978.

COLES, Robert, "Children and Political Authority," T. B. Davis Memorial Lecture, Capetown: August 27, 1974.

CONNELL, R. W., *The Child's Construction of Politics*, Carlton, Victoria: Melbourne University Press, 1971.

DREITZL, Hans Peter (ed.), *Childhood and Socialization*, New York: Macmillian, 1973.

GREENBERG, Edward S. (ed.), *Political Socialization*, New York: Lieber-Atherton, 1973.

GREENSTEIN, Fred I., *Children and Politics*, New Haven: Yale University Press, 1965.

NIEMI, Richard G. and Associates, *The Politics of Future Citizens*, San Francisco: Jossey-Bass Publishers, 1974.

SCHRAG, Francis, "The Child's Status in the Democratic State," *Political Theory*, v.3, n.4. 1975.

JUVENILE JUSTICE

COLE, Larry, *Our Children's Keepers*, New York: Ballentine Books, 1972.

FOUST, Frederic L. and Paul J. Brantingham (eds.), *Juvenile Justice Philosophy*, St. Paul: West Publishing Co., 1974.

FORER, Lois G., *"No One Will Listen,"* New York: Grosset & Dunlap, 1970.

INTERNATIONAL PRISON COMMISSION, *Children's Courts in the United States*, Washington, D.C.: Government Printing Office, 1904.

JUDGE BAKER FOUNDATION, *Harvey Humphrey Baker: Upholder of the Juvenile Court*, Boston: Judge Baker Foundation, 1920.

LENERT, Edwin M., *Instead of Court*, Chevy Chase, MD.: National Institute of Mental Health, 1971.

MENNEL, Robert M., *Thorns and Thistles*, Hanover, N.H.: The University Press of New England, 1973.

ROSENHEIM, Margaret K. (ed.), *Pursuing Justice for the Child*, Chicago: University of Chicago Press, 1976.

SCHUR, Edwin M., *Radical Non-Intervention*, Englewood Cliffs, N.J.: Prentice-Hall, 1973.

STAPLETON, W. Vaughan and Lee E. Teitlebaum, *In Defense of Youth*, New York: Russell Sage Foundation, 1972.

WOODEN, Kenneth, *Weeping in the Playtime of Others*, New York: McGraw-Hill, 1976.

PRIVACY RIGHTS AND CHILDREN

BRECKENRIDGE, Adam, *The Right to Privacy*, Lincoln, Nb.: University of Nebraska Press, 1970.

CLARKE, Lorenne M. G., "Privacy, Property, Freedom and the Family," *Philosophical Law*, Westport, Conn.: Greenwood Press, 1978.

COHEN, Howard, "Children and Privacy," in Richard Bronaugh (ed.), *Philosophical Law*, Westport, Conn.: Greenwood Press, 1978.

ERNST, Morris and Alan Schwartz, *Privacy: The Right to Be Let Alone*, London: MacGibbon and Kee, 1968.

GREENAWALT, Kent, *Legal Protections of Privacy*, Washington, D.C.: U.S. Government Printing Office, 1975.

MAYER, Michael, *Rights of Privacy*, New York: Law-Arts Publishers, Inc., 1972.

WESTIN, Alan, *Privacy and Freedom*, New York: Atheneum, 1967.

Index

Index